EUROPE
AT THE OUTBREAK OF WORLD WAR I
AUGUST 1914

FINLAND

elsinfors

Reval

Riga

St. Petersburg (Petrograd)

Novgorod

Moscow

Smolensk

Kovno

Vilna

R   U   S   S   I   A

Bryansk

Orel

Voronezh

POLAND

Pinsk

Kursk

Brest·Litovsk

Kiev

Kharkov

Lemberg

GALICIA

DNIEPER

DNIESTER

DON

VOLGA

VOLGA

OKA

BUG

Rostov

CASPIAN
SEA

GARY

TRANSYLVANIA

BESSARABIA

PRUT

Odessa

RUMANIA

Bucharest

DANUBE

BLACK SEA

Tiflis

Baku

Batum

BULGARIA

Sofia

Constantinople

T   U   R   K   E   Y

Tabriz

PERSIA

lonika

ECE

Athens

Smyrna

Angora

HALYS

MESOPOTAMIA

Baghdad

SYRIA

CRETE

CYPRUS

Damascus

PALESTINE

ARABIA

MILES 0 — 300
KM 0 — 300

palacios

A Pictorial History of the
WORLD WAR 1 YEARS

A PICTORIAL HISTORY OF

THE
WORLD WAR 1
YEARS

EDWARD JABLONSKI

Maps by Rafael Palacios

DOUBLEDAY & COMPANY, Inc.
Garden City, New York

LIBRARY OF CONGRESS CATALOG CARD NUMBER 78–20639

9 8 7 6 5 4

Library of Congress Cataloging in Publication Data

Jablonski, Edward.
A pictorial history of the World War I years.

Includes index.
1. European War, 1914-1918.   I.   Title.
D521.J18   940.3   78-20639
ISBN: 0-385-18552-9

For my sister Mary,
who has been through the wars.

Contents

AUTHOR'S NOTE

MARY SHERWIN, editor, did virtually all of the photo research for this volume besides checking (gently) now and then on the work in progress—and then putting it into printable form. We are both grateful to Cyrus Rogers for his careful, and knowledgeable, copy editing.

We are grateful also for assistance received from various sources—particularly the Imperial War Museum, London, and to E. C. Hine, an old friend of other wars, and to Keeper of the Photographs, R. E. K. Crawford. Another friend-aide, Paul White, courteously guided us (Mary, rather) through the labyrinths of our richly stocked National Archives in Washington, D.C.

Other picture sources include the French Embassy Press and Information Services, New York; the United States Air Force, Washington, D.C.; Austrian Information Service, Vienna; German Information Service, New York; the New York Public Library Picture Collection; Etablissement Cinématographique des Armées, Fort d'Ivry, France. Many illustrations were acquired years ago through the generosity of the late Colonel G. G. Jarrett, military historian, Aberdeen, Maryland. Other sources are noted with each illustration.

My especial thanks to my sister-in-law, Barbara Garson Busch, who presented me with an invaluable collection of firsthand materials about the war—the full history and documentation as seen by the participants at the time and shortly after the war ended. Without the documentation it would have been difficult indeed to track down many a spelling and incident all but lost to history.

A final word on the section titles, all of which are also the titles of songs popular during the war. Unlike any war before or since, the "Great War" inspired (if that's the word) many long-lasting songs. These often accurately expressed popular sentiment and attitudes. When the war began they were exuberant, even lighthearted, and, as the war continued, they grew pessimistic, somber, and cynical as it became obvious that all too frequently a march merely preceded a requiem.

E.J.

A Pictorial History of the WORLD WAR 1 YEARS

Causes of World War 1

To MOST of the participants World War I was known as the Great War; some even believed it was the "war to end war." It was not, in fact, even a true world war, but the prelude to one. Numbering mankind's "world" wars began long after the Great War was over and the Versailles Treaty—as we know now and they did not know then—assured the advent of the future real world war.

World War I did not evolve as those who were responsible for it—who fought in it—imagined, hoped, or dreamed. What began as a nationalistic lark soon metamorphosed into a grim nightmare—history's most haunting war (excepting perhaps Vietnam). Zealous, confident armies marched to the battlefronts to the ardent cheering of their fellow countrymen and women right out of the romanticism of the nineteenth century into the realism of the twentieth. Not only armies but cherished concepts crumbled, among them empires, monarchies, generals, and war itself.

Wars, invariably, are led by elderly men with set ideas on how things should be done. The aristocrats and gentlemen who commanded the great armies—and there had never been such numbers before—were traditionalists. They took their cues from the classic textbooks and words of revered military thinkers, long dead like their ideas. They even called it *the art* of warfare, consisting of grand strategies on paper, artillery barrages, cavalry charges, marching infantrymen. Ignored was the human propensity, an ingenuity, for devising new destructive weapons under pressure—unheard-of innovations during the previous war. World War I unleashed such battlefield surprises as poison gas and the machine gun (not new, of course, but never so widely and devastatingly before); tanks, submarines under the sea, and various types of aircraft in the sky were also used. Not the least was the stalemate of static trench

Kaiser Wilhelm II, World War I's chief scapegoat. Maneuvered into war, he was eventually blamed for it. Here he talks to a German officer at a party. In the background: General Paul von Hindenburg and the German Crown Prince Wilhelm, who, because of the war's final outcome, never became III.

warfare on the Western Front. Such nonclassical slaughter techniques were undreamed of in the philosophies of the determined mature men who led their nations' youth into the war of 1914–1918.

The favorite villain of World War I was Germany's Kaiser, Wilhelm II. He was not, in fact, responsible for the outbreak of the war; he merely stood by and let it happen and, once it did, he kept it going. Germany was the major military power in Europe in 1914; the Kaiser's position on any military question was weighty indeed. As for the high seas, Germany was second only to the great maritime power, Britain. Wilhelm II, a vain, arrogant, mercurial man, reveled in power and wielded it with an erratic lack of thought; the greater consequences of a petty decision did not concern him. Born with a shrunken arm (the result of a midwife's error at his birth), Wilhelm II was sorely conscious of the defect, generally hid it, and compensated with belligerent talk, an admiration for and the desire to emulate Frederick the Great. The Kaiser liked the military and its display (the colorful uniforms served to screen his withered arm), which easily placed him under the sway of his military advisers and out of touch with diplomats and statesmen.

The true, basic cause of the war (in simple terms) was nationalism complicated by an intricate system of alliances. The smoldering Balkans provided the incendiary setting. The Serbian Government was determined to liberate those Serbs under the domination of Austria-Hungary (an ally of Germany). The Russians, sympathetic to the plight of their fellow Slavs, were, in turn, allied with France—still seething over the German annexation of Alsace-Lorraine in 1871. Britain, meanwhile, kept a wary sea dog's eye on Germany's expanding navy and a worried eye on restive Ireland. It was a matter of family rivalry: the Kaiser was a cousin to King George V.

Another cousin, tyrannical Czar Nicholas II of Imperial Russia, whose regime was described as a "tangle of cowardice, blindness, craftiness and stupidity," ruled a great nation under the sway of a mad, self-styled holy man, Grigori Rasputin. The Czar chose to ignore his country's political-social unrest; in exile, two dissidents—Leon Trotsky and Nikolai Lenin—waited for something to happen.

The two blustering, bumbling cousins, the Kaiser and the Czar (their common relative, incidentally, had been Queen Victoria), helped bring about the hostilities; they were caught up in a series of minor events, social and political forces they could never begin to understand.

A nineteen-year-old student provided them with the incident. Gavrilo Princip was a member of a secret nationalistic movement, Mlada Bosna

National Archives

Nicholas II, Czar of Russia, inspecting his troops. Neither a great emperor nor a great general, Nicholas and his regime would not last out the war.

End of the line: Archduke Franz Ferdinand and Emperor Franz Joseph of Austria, without, as usual, the Archduke's wife Sophie. The Archduke died before the war began and the Emperor died before it ended. European royalty appears to have been addicted to military uniforms during this period.

("Young Bosnia"), dedicated to freeing the Balkans of the Hapsburg yoke. He was one of seven youthful would-be assassins furnished with weapons, hand grenades, guns, and ammunition by a Serbian terrorist organization called the "Black Hand." Princip and company were to attempt to kill Archduke Franz Ferdinand, who was scheduled to make a visit with his wife to the Bosnian capital, Sarajevo, on June 28, 1914.

The Archduke was a nephew of Austrian Emperor Franz Joseph and heir to the throne of Austria-Hungary; in 1914 his uncle was over eighty years old, the self-styled "last monarch of the old school." Several members of his family had met with unnatural deaths, while he had been spared. The Emperor's brother Maximilian was executed in Mexico; his son Rudolf romantically committed suicide in Mayerling; and his wife,

Elizabeth, had been assassinated by an anarchist in Geneva. When the Emperor visited Sarajevo in 1910, the streets were lined with a double cordon of troops. Such precaution was not taken at the time of the Archduke's ill-timed visit in 1914.

The trip was an act of double defiance. Not only had the Archduke elected to come to Sarajevo on the day of the St. Vitus Festival, commemorating the Battle of Kosovo (June 28, 1389, when the Serbs suffered a terrible defeat at the hands of their traditional enemies, the Turks), but he also brought his wife along. June 28 happened to be their fourteenth wedding anniversary.

The Emperor regarded the marriage as unfortunate; Countess Sophie, Duchess of Hohenberg, was not of royal blood and was thus beneath his nephew's station. It took a year of argument to persuade Franz Joseph to accept the marriage—but at the cost of denying any children of the marriage the right of succession to the throne. Sophie could not even ride beside her husband in the royal coach on state occasions; she was snubbed in court.

The Sarajevo trip was for military, not state, reasons. As Inspector General of the Army, the Archduke was invited to a viewing of the maneuvers of the Austrian Army in the vicinity of Sarajevo. On this occasion Sophie, with full honors, could ride beside her husband. Theirs was the second in a four-car motorcade that passed through the hostile,

Sarajevo, 1914. Countess Sophie and Archduke Franz Ferdinand about to enter their death car.

Gavrilo Princip in custody after the assassination that ignited World War I. Photo reproduced from a contemporary newspaper.

meagerly guarded streets. Warnings had come, literally, from embassies all over the world that had heard trouble was expected. They were ignored. The Austrian troops were not permitted to enter the town and police precautions were little better than routine. The first indication that the warnings had substance occurred when a hand grenade arched out of the crowd and hurtled at the motorcade. The Archduke, in protectively placing his arm around his wife, deflected the grenade from their car and into the street. Twenty people were injured by the blast, including three from the royal party. Sophie was slightly injured in the neck by a flying splinter.

Although the speed of the motorcade was increased, the original plan of the visit was not abandoned. The Military Governor, General Oskar Potiorek, assured the shaken, angry Archduke: "Your Imperial Highness, you can travel quite happily. I take the responsibility."

As the cars raced toward the City Hall, the motorcade slipped past three potential assassins, unable to act because of the speed of the vehicles and because they were caught off guard.

18

After the City Hall ceremony, the Archduke expressed a wish to visit the hospital on the return trip to see those who had been hospitalized by the earlier attempt on his life. The driver of the car, confused or misinformed, made a wrong turn, away from the correct route and back to the scheduled itinerary (passing by yet another surprised, ineffectual assassin).

On this street, named for the Emperor Franz Joseph, was the consumptive Gavrilo Princip, awaiting the royal motorcade with a gun. He stood only five feet from the Archduke's car when the driver stopped to make a turn. As the Emperor chastised the driver, Princip fired twice. General Potiorek, who had taken "the responsibility," checked on his charges, both of whom appeared to be seated calmly, and ordered the driver to continue on. Suddenly a stream of blood gushed from the Archduke's mouth and his wife screamed, "For heaven's sake, what's happened to you?" She then collapsed, Potiorek was certain, in a faint.

What he did not know was that the bullet aimed at himself had struck Sophie in the stomach and the other bullet the neck of the Archduke, severing the jugular vein and lodging in his spine. Both were fatally wounded. His wife was already dead when the Archduke pleaded, "Sophie dear, Sophie dear, don't die! Stay alive for our children." By 11:30 A.M. both were dead.

Princip, meanwhile, was seized by the police. An attempt at suicide with the murder gun failed when a bystander knocked the weapon from Princip's hand. He tried suicide again by swallowing cyanide, but it made him ill and he vomited the poison. Princip lived to stand trial and was found guilty but, because of his youth, escaped the death penalty. Consumed by tuberculosis, Princip died in prison in 1918—the same year in which the great war he unknowingly ignited sputtered out.

The haunting question remains: why should the death of two obscure, not especially popular individuals—only one of whom could claim royal blood—lead to four years of the worst slaughter the world had known to that time? Beyond their quite touching personal relationship, the Archduke and his socially abused morganatic wife meant little to the great political-military thinkers of the moment. Alive, they hardly belonged on the world's stage; dead, they were cast as stars in a great drama.

Their corpses served beautifully in the plans of the military clique in Vienna. Having lost their former leader, the Archduke, they pressed even harder for a little punitive war, which they had been advocating for years, to teach the discontented, disruptive Serbs a lesson. Although an investigation following the assassination in Sarajevo revealed no link between the assassins and the Serbian Government, the war party in Vienna, under General Franz Conrad von Hötzendorf, Chief of the Austro-Hungarian General Staff, refused to accept the result of the findings. His view was that the assassination of the Archduke was "not the crime

Chief of the Austro-Hungarian General Staff, General Franz Conrad von Hötzendorf, who was undoubtedly more responsible for World War I than the hapless Kaiser.

of a single fanatic; assassination represents Serbia's declaration of war on Austria-Hungary . . . If we miss this occasion, the monarchy will be exposed to new explosions of South Slav, Czech, Russian, Rumanian and Italian aspirations. Austria-Hungary must wage war for political reasons."

Despite further confirmation of the innocence of the Serbian Government by a special investigative group of the Foreign Ministry in Vienna (and agreement with the findings in Berlin), Conrad, in concert with

20

the Foreign Minister, Count Leopold von Berchtold, continued to press for his little war on Serbia.

Because Princip and the other assassins had been provided with weapons and explosives by the Black Hand (which in fact was in conflict with the Serbian Government), Conrad and Berchtold used that as a pretext for dispatching an ultimatum to the Serbs. Other facts—that Princip was not a Serbian, but a Bosnian; that two investigations had not succeeded in implicating the Serbian Government—were disregarded. Certain men had initiated a sequence of what appeared to be minor events, but these events very quickly enveloped and mastered them.

Austria delivered a memorandum to Serbia on July 23, not quite a month after the murders. There were ten curtly worded demands; the Serbs were agreeable and even conciliatory, accepting all but one.

Diplomat Count Leopold von Berchtold, Austro-Hungarian Foreign Minister, who conspired with Conrad von Hötzendorf in "a little war."

Berchtold's draft of the declaration of war on Serbia.

Demand No. 6, it was explained—which would have permitted the Viennese domination of a Serbian court of law—violated the Serbian Constitution and the law of criminal procedure. The Serbs respectfully replied: perhaps the point could be further discussed before The Hague Court of Arbitration. The reply was sent on July 25.

Meanwhile, although cautioning the Serbs not to put up any resistance should there be an Austro-Hungarian invasion, the Russians began mobilizing troops within striking distance of Austria-Hungary. This was heartening to the Serbs. So was the fact that Berlin had found the Serbian reply to Vienna a reasonable one.

There was no placating the little military group in Vienna; aided by the duplicity and incompetence of Berchtold (who seems to have lied to every crowned head in Europe), they had their way. On July 28 the Foreign Ministry in Vienna informed the Serbian Government by telegram (a historic first) that, as of 11 A.M., a state of war existed between Austria-Hungary and Serbia. It was signed by Count Leopold von Berchtold. He hadn't bothered to inform Kaiser Wilhelm, still rejoicing over the Serbian reply to the original ultimatum. "A great moral victory for Vienna," he had called it. And with it, he felt, "every reason for war disappears." Berchtold proved him wrong.

The declaration of war, however much it surprised the Kaiser, was even more disturbing to his cousin Czar Nicholas in St. Petersburg (now Leningrad). He considered at least partial mobilization to go to the aid of his fellow Slavs. A series of friendly "Nicky" and "Willy" telegrams passed between St. Petersburg and Berlin. Perhaps the little war could be contained. But the Russian call for mobilization angered Cousin Willy, who refused further attempts at mediation. In a temper tantrum he declared, "My work is at an end!"

Cousin Nicky, who had been vacillating by permitting only a partial mobilization, had his own tantrum. When one of his military advisers, commiserating over the pressures of decision-making upon the Czar, said, "It is hard to decide," Nicholas II snapped, "I will decide!"—and he did, on July 30, ordering a full general mobilization.

In Berlin the mobilization of a nation that was not an ally meant war, an axiom inherited from the admired late Chief of the German General Staff, General Count Alfred von Schlieffen, who had died only the year before. His dead hand would be much in evidence in the days to come. If the Russians were mobilizing in the east, did that mean perhaps Russia's ally in the west, France, was also mobilizing? Either Russia must be stopped or Germany, which had not begun any mobilization, must strike first. On July 31, Germany sent an ultimatum to Russia demanding Russian demobilization within twelve hours. The Russians refused.

On August 1, 1914, Germany declared war on Russia and ordered a general mobilization. On the same day France initiated its general mobilization. Meanwhile, the belligerent Austro-Hungarian Army had not yet begun to move into Serbia—and would not for another ten days, during which time most of Europe would become entangled in a great war merely because of "another Balkan quarrel," as it was regarded in Great Britain.

23

Germany's plans shifted the center of interest away from the Balkans —the first objective of the German General Staff was France. To bypass practically impregnable fortifications along their common frontier, Germany would have to send its troops through Belgium. In 1839 both Germany and Britain had signed a document guaranteeing Belgium's neutrality and borders. When on August 2 German troops violated the neutrality of Luxembourg at the southeast tip of Belgium, it was obvious what the next move would be. The London government grew restive; the thought of a warlike Germany just across the English Channel was an unpleasant prospect.

On August 3, Germany declared war on France and began the invasion of neutral Belgium. King Albert appealed to Britain for support. Even at this juncture it might have been possible to curb hostilities. The Kaiser was ready to cancel the Luxembourg invasion upon hearing that Britain might persuade France to remain neutral if the invasion of Belgium were canceled. But once the machinery of invasion, involving a

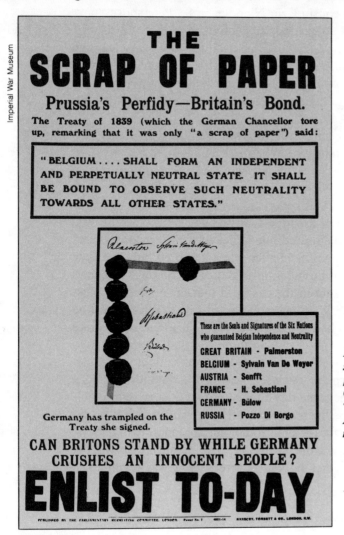

Imperial War Museum

Recruiting poster reproducing the signatures of the treaty of 1839 promising Belgian neutrality. The German Chancellor dismissed it as "a scrap of paper," presenting the Allies with good propaganda material.

The old: the commanders were invariably aged, wore the uniforms of the last war, and favored its weapons and techniques. The youth of the nation died to prove them wrong. Hindenburg, who came out of retirement to participate in the war (far right), points out one of his weighty medals.

million men, had begun to move, there was no stopping it. Besides, the Kaiser's generals ignored his suggestion regarding Luxembourg and the invasion of small neutral countries proceeded.

On August 4, London communicated its ultimatum to Berlin. German Chancellor Theobald von Bethmann-Hollweg was aghast. "How," he demanded of the British Ambassador, "could Britain go to war over a scrap of paper?" This was the 1839 agreement signed by Britain and Germany.

25

The old and the new: a prewar military maneuver in which members of the traditional branch, the British cavalry, observe with apprehensive suspicion one of the newer weapons of war drifting by—a B.E.2B.

The invasion of "little Belgium" was not halted. That evening Britain declared war on Germany. It appeared as if suddenly, for reasons difficult to pinpoint, all of Europe—from the Atlantic to the vast wastelands of Russia—was embroiled in war. The dead Archduke and Sophie had long been forgotten, lost in the shuffling of paper, misunderstandings, clashing personalities, and a confusion of ultimatums and declarations. The British Foreign Secretary, Sir Edward Grey, misled as much as anyone by the overlapping concatenation of events no longer controlled by men, viewed the shambles of military diplomacy with poetic foreboding.

"The lamps are going out all over Europe," he said, "we shall not see them lit again in our lifetime."

1914

"Oh, What a Lovely War!"

THE British Foreign Secretary's gloominess was not evident in other war capitals of Europe while their troops were marching off to war. While the Austrian Army, whose commander had instigated it all, prepared for a full-scale invasion of Serbia and the Russian mass general mobilization ground into cumbrous motion, a holiday mood infected Paris and Berlin. French and German military leaders were confident that the war would be over by autumn and each army would soon be in the enemy capital. German troops, in field uniforms and the classic spiked helmets, were cheered by enthusiastic crowds in their march toward Paris. Women presented soldiers with flowers and marched arm in arm; civilian men joined the parade too, assisting in carrying the heavy Mauser rifles. With jubilation engulfing them, a million and a half men set out for Paris; another half million proceeded to the Eastern Front to contain the Russians until Paris fell.

The mood in Paris, though more subdued than in Berlin, was one of cheerful optimism. "Crowds were gathered at every [railroad] station, behind every barrier, and at every window along our road," recalled one Commandant A. Grasset. "Cries of *'Vive la France! Vive l'armée!'* could be heard everywhere, while people waved handkerchiefs and hats. The women were throwing kisses and heaped flowers upon our convoy."

The marching French columns, bedecked with flowers, were impressively dashing and, indeed, colorful in their gay red trousers (*"Le pantalon rouge c'est la France!"*). To the joyous strains of *La Marseillaise* the vivacious French Army, exulting in its famed élan ("Attack, attack, always attack"), set off for Berlin. With less élan perhaps, but with music in their ears, similarly garlanded and cheered, the German Army continued on toward Paris.

The two greatest military powers in Europe had prepared two master plans for the speedy victory each expected to gain. Neither, like so many grand strategies, worked.

The German plan dated back to 1905, the brainchild of the Chief of the German General Staff, Count Alfred von Schlieffen; its major feature was an attack on France through Belgium. The plan was modified by Schlieffen's successor, General Helmuth von Moltke, but not significantly in so far as violating the neutrality of Belgium was concerned. The plan's main point was to get German troops into France, Paris being a major objective, by avoiding all possible natural obstacles and taking advantage of modern transportation systems. The plan did not take into account the possibility that the German Army might face the Russian Army on a second front.

Execution of the Schlieffen Plan, with variations, fell to the ailing and aging (he was sixty-six) Moltke, who had little stomach for a real war. For years he had lived in the shadow of his uncle, also a Helmuth von Moltke, who had the distinction of having been the first Chief of the German General Staff and the admired author of several victorious strategies. Whether it was a sign of his own insecurity or a spark of reality is now academic, but Moltke saw the war only as the promise of a long and wearisome struggle.

Marching as to war: Berliners join in the celebration of the declaration of war.

French troops leaving for the front, most of them to the wrong one in Lorraine. The major German invasion was planned for farther north.

The French strategy (Plan XVII) was simplicity itself: a headlong rush, with all due élan, into the center of the German armies. The French General Staff expected that the German attack would be concentrated in Lorraine, through northeastern France. What the French plan did not take into account was the German plan (which would send the concentration of German troops through Belgium into northeastern France). The French thinking was dominated by *les jeunes Turcs* and its "School of Attack." One of its prime philosophers, Lieutenant Colonel Louzeau de Grandmaison, said it all when he stated, "For the attack only two things are necessary: to know where the enemy is and to decide what to do. What the enemy intends to do is of no consequence."

30

Special edition of a Berlin newspaper announcing
Germany's declaration of war on France.

What the enemy had intended to do was not to be where the French "knew" they would be. Even as it became evident during the early weeks of the war that the mass of the German invasion was moving through Belgium, French commander General Joseph Joffre obstinately followed his Plan XVII.

It was not that the Schlieffen-Moltke Plan was a masterpiece that might have checkmated Plan XVII; rather, it appears as if the two plans were conceived for different wars. Some military scholars argue that, had Moltke been less chickenhearted and followed the original Schlieffen Plan (which also included an invasion of neutral Holland), he might have gained an early victory. He had subtracted troops from

*The second Helmuth von Moltke, nephew of the first and German
Chief of Staff when the war for which he had no stomach came.*

the major invasion force to place two divisions facing the French right
flank in Lorraine; he also sacrificed some of his forces to the Eastern
Front to assist the Austrians in holding off the slowly mobilizing Russians.

Within six weeks, Moltke hoped, the war on the Western Front would
be over; five armies would sweep through Belgium into France, swing
around short of the English Channel, and, after encircling Paris, push
eastward to crush the main French forces, complying with Plan XVII,
from the rear in Lorraine. Some military theoreticians contend that this
was possible; some insist that it was not. Some historians brand Moltke a
bumbler and others the scapegoat of the plan's predestined failure: all,
of course, profound hindsight.

The initial invasion, first through tiny (therefore insignificant) Luxembourg, then through Belgium, was intended to avoid the heavily
fortified Franco-German border. On Sunday, August 2, 1914, having
declared war on Russia the day before, Germany moved into Luxem-

32

bourg to assure rail transportation into France. On August 3, Germany declared war on France. The fact of Luxembourg's occupation seemed lost on the French High Command. So was the ultimatum demanding free passage of German troops through Belgium. During the morning of August 4 advance forces of the German Army began moving into Belgium—a move that brought Great Britain into the war.

Although Belgium had never before fought in a war, it was not a tiny helpless Luxembourg; a key position in the way of the invading Germans was the Liège and Namur fortifications which would have to be breached before Moltke's forces could move on to Brussels and into France. The small Belgian Army, hoping for quick help from Britain and France, held. Aroused Belgian civilians sniped at the invaders; it was not like Luxembourg at all.

This unexpected resistance was met with savage retaliation. "Our advance in Belgium is certainly brutal," Moltke admitted, "but we are fighting for our lives and all who get in the way must take the consequences." Shocked and frightened by sniping Belgians, the Germans lashed out with savage vindictiveness, shooting and burning soldier and civilian alike. The American Minister in Belgium, Brand Whitlock, reported to the Secretary of State, "Towns were sacked and burned, homes were pillaged; in many places portions of the population, men, women and children, were massed in public squares and mowed down by *mitrailleuses* [machine guns], and there were countless individual instances of an amazing and shameless brutality."

Aside from such instances—and there were plenty—were the horrible accounts provided by rumor and propaganda: the infamous Belgian atrocity stories. These included mass public rape, church burnings, cutting off the hands of children, bayoneting children in their mothers' arms, and cutting off the breasts of young women (often as not, it was reported that these victims were nuns). While most of these propaganda tales were proved false, long after the war ended, the fact is that the German push through Belgium left about five thousand civilians dead and burned-out towns and villages in its wake.

When the warring began, Moltke dispatched his Eighth Army, under the command of Colonel General Max von Prittwitz und Gaffron, to detain the Russians while Belgium and France, and whatever British forces were there, were finished off on the Western Front. He assigned two armies the job of keeping the French preoccupied: the Sixth, commanded by Crown Prince Rupprecht of Bavaria; and the Seventh, under General Josias von Heeringen, on the extreme left of the German front opposite two French armies designated to execute Plan XVII in Lorraine.

The major German striking force consisted of five armies: at the extreme right was the First Army, commanded by General Alexander von Kluck, which was to smash through Belgium and northern France be-

The professionals: General Alexander von Kluck (wearing a greatcoat) and his staff. Kluck commanded the German First Army, which invaded Belgium.

fore swinging around south of Paris. To Kluck's left was the Second Army (General Karl von Bülow), to Bülow's left, the Third Army (General Max Klemens von Hausen). The Fourth Army was commanded by Albrecht, Duke of Württemberg, and the Fifth by the Kaiser's son, Crown Prince Wilhelm. This collection of stiff-necked professional soldiers, political officers, and royalty (Wilhelm, the Prince, was ultimately responsible only to his father) did not make for a smoothly running war machine. The two professionals, Kluck and Bülow, shared a contempt for Moltke and for each other.

The concerned American, reading the New York *Times* on August 6, 1914, just two days after the invasion of Belgium, was led to believe that all was going well for the Allies. "Belgians Defeat Germans, Kill or Wound 3,500 Men," the top line of the front page headline read. Also: "Russians Drive Out Germans and Enter Prussia . . ." Such good news, at least to those sympathetic to the Allies, continued to come for several days, especially from the Western Front.

Meanwhile, the German armies had begun their assault on the fortress city of Liège. The Belgian commander, General Gérard Leman, ordered by King Albert "to hold to the end," complied with those orders. This unexpected resistance upset the German timetable and left many German corpses in the bloody Meuse River. This disruption produced Germany's first great hero of the war: Colonel (very soon he became General) Erich Ludendorff, a staff officer of the Second Army. When the commander of the 14th Brigade, which Ludendorff joined temporarily as an observer, was killed, Ludendorff took over and led the German attackers into the inner citadel of Liège; on August 17 the city itself was taken.

But the forts around Liège continued to hold out. Leman, aware of German cavalry penetrations between the forts, abandoned Liège and moved his own headquarters to Fort Roncin. Hero Ludendorff had, in effect, cut off the 14th Brigade from the rest of X Corps (of Bülow's Second Army). The commander of X Corps, General Otto von Emmich, imprisoned also inside Liège, fought his way out by August 10 and took Fort Barchon from the rear. A neighboring fort fell to other German troops and cleared the way to bring up the 420-mm. siege guns. The obsolescent forts ringing Liège were dealt with one by one until, finally, on August 15, General Leman himself was pulled, unconscious but alive, from the debris of Fort Roncin. The remaining forts surrendered the next day; the road to the Marne was open.

The invasion of Belgium brought the promised aid from Britain: the small (about a hundred thousand strong) but very professional British Expeditionary Force under the command of Field Marshal Sir John French. French arrived in France on August 14, even as the big German guns were reducing the forts around Liège. The Royal Navy, without interference from the German Navy, ferried the B.E.F. into Le Havre. While Field Marshal French socialized in Paris—he was impressed with

Two who dominated German military fortunes through most of the war. Paul von Hindenburg (left), who took command of the Eastern Front, and Erich von Ludendorff, who became an instant hero during the invasion of Belgium—and who did most of Hindenburg's thinking for him.

the French Commander-in-Chief, Marshal Joseph Joffre—the units of the B.E.F. moved into Belgium and formed a front in the neighborhood of the Mons–Condé canal by August 20. On the British right was the French Fifth Army, under General Charles Lanrezac. Sir John was not much impressed with his neighbor, who, when they met, offered the opinion, "At last you're here; it's not a moment too soon. If we are beaten we will owe it all to you."

Studying a situation map, Sir John asked Lanrezac, "What are the Germans doing on the Meuse River?"

"What are they doing there? Why, fishing, of course," was Lanrezac's caustic reply (which was not translated for the English field marshal). It was not necessary; Lanrezac's expression and the map markings were enough for Sir John; he soon lost some of his enthusiasm for the war.

In Belgium, although the Germans occupied Brussels, the remnants of the Belgian Army found refuge in heavily fortified Antwerp. This stand tied up some of Kluck's forces while, minus these troops, he pushed through Belgium, practically on schedule. On August 20, the day the B.E.F. approached Mons, Moltke ordered the fortress city of Namur to be placed under siege, for he had information that only seven or eight French corps of the Fifth Army stood in his way. As for the British and their promised aid to Belgium and France, he informed his commanders, "It is the view here that no important debarkations have so far taken place."

By August 21, brave *poilus* of Lanrezac's Fifth Army were being slaughtered by the vanguard of Bülow's Second Army. Charging with bayonets into heavy machine-gun fire canceled out all the élan in the world and thousands of young French lives. The Belgians were forced to evacuate Namur and, though it held (it would surrender the first week in September), Lanrezac's troops fell back before the tide of field gray. Lanrezac neglected to inform French that the withdrawal of his forces left the British right flank exposed.

On Sunday, August 23, the Germans ran directly into the army that wasn't supposed to be there: the British Expeditionary Force. Kluck was hoping to outflank Lanrezac; he knew that the British had landed, but thought they were thirty miles away, at Tournai. The confrontation at Mons was a general surprise to all.

The British were heavily outnumbered, but initially their professionalism took its toll. Rifle fire was so rapid that the Germans were certain they had run into machine guns (which, in fact, for the moment, the British High Command did not consider a proper weapon for a professional army). The British held their positions until the full pressure of German numbers—and severe British losses—told. By the next morning the British began withdrawing from Mons. They had two very good reasons: German superiority in numbers and the knowledge that Lanre-

General Joseph Joffre, French Commander-in-Chief, and his military aide,
Ferdinand Foch, who distinguished himself during the early months of the
war. By the war's end he would have Joffre's job.

zac, without informing them, had pulled out his Fifth Army. With no
troops to his left and with Lanrezac leaving his right exposed, Sir John
French ordered the B.E.F. to pull back from Mons. What had been
regarded as a British victory had changed to defeat. French informed his
chief, the newly appointed Secretary of State for War, Field Marshal
Lord Horatio Kitchener, that getting out of the battle zone altogether
was not a bad idea.

The retreat continued, although Kitchener quickly changed French's
mind about a total retreat. On August 26, the harried British II Corps
(General Sir Horace Smith-Dorrien), partly exhausted and partly
refreshed by the arrival of a new division from Britain, decided to take a
stand at Le Cateau, some thirty miles southwest of Mons. This was ac-

37

German ammunition wagons in Brussels, heading for the Marne.

complished at great cost to both sides, although the British were considerably outnumbered by the Germans. Tired French troops also joined the British in checking the German advance.

By evening the British were in retreat again and Kluck was certain he had thoroughly defeated them; he was equally certain that the survivors were fleeing to the southwest and he ordered his First Army in pursuit. His quarry eluded him, for the British had withdrawn through difficult country of wooded hills to the south.

Still, with the French in retreat on all fronts also, Kluck had reason for optimistically expecting a "decisive victory." On August 30 the rumble of German guns could be heard in Paris; a Taube monoplane, Maltese crosses on its wings, appeared over Paris as early as August 13, to drop a few ineffectual bombs. (Dispatches reported "two women wounded.") By August 30 leaflets fluttered onto the streets of Paris with the headline: "PEOPLE OF PARIS! SURRENDER! The Germans are at your gates! You can do nothing but surrender."

The sound of enemy guns confirmed the fears of Parisians and their panicking government. German aircraft flew over the city at will, it seemed, and there appeared to be no stopping the oncoming German horde. On August 31 the French Government headed for Bordeaux, leaving sixty-five-year-old General Joseph Gallieni behind as Military Governor of Paris.

Gallieni seemed an unlikely choice for the role of savior; a wizened little man, he was unmilitary in dress, sported a shaggy mustache and a pince-nez. The British were thoroughly unimpressed. "No British officer," one said, "would be seen speaking to such a comedian."

Five German armies pressed toward Paris, pushing Joffre's and

French's tired troops before them. Gallieni, who had once been Joffre's commanding officer and was disturbed by his imperturbability, acted quickly. As Joffre vacillated, Gallieni began improving the long-neglected defenses of Paris with barricades and trenches; he had various bridges leading into Paris mined with explosives—even the Eiffel Tower could be detonated if the Germans reached the city.

Gallieni stocked the parks and racetracks with livestock in case Paris came under siege (a previous siege necessitated the depletion of Paris zoos and the slaughter of pets for food). His most dramatic contribution was to commandeer hundreds of Paris taxicabs—the famous "Taxis of the Marne"—to transport fresh troops to the battlefront.

Joffre finally bestirred himself long enough to form a new army—the Sixth, under the command of General Michel Maunoury. He did this by borrowing a division from Alsace on the French right (the only experienced fighting unit), and adding three green reserve divisions and, later (as the Germans approached Paris even closer), a tough Algerian division and Moroccan troops. The main mission of the Sixth Army was to defend Paris. Joffre made yet another decision: he relieved Lanrezac of his command and turned the Fifth Army over to General Louis Franchet d'Esperey. He assigned Lanrezac to serve under the aggressive Gallieni, warning his old commander of Lanrezac's predisposition: "You must not pay any attention to his pessimism, which makes him see only the risks involved in an operation and paralyzes his initiative . . ."

Moltke, certain that he had the Allies on the run and near defeat, released four divisions to the Eastern Front (where they arrived too late to contribute to the fighting), and weakened his right wing on the Western Front. Kluck, instead of swinging westward in keeping with the

39

Schlieffen Plan, began moving south, which brought his First Army to the east of Paris. This decision created a gap between his army and Bülow's Second.

A French plane over the battlefront spotted the Germans moving southward toward Paris. While Maunoury's new Sixth Army engaged Kluck's left flank, the B.E.F. and the French Sixth Army moved toward the gap between Kluck's and Bülow's armies. Maunoury's appeal for reinforcements was met by the resourceful Gallieni on September 5, when he requisitioned "all self-propelled vehicles, including taxicabs," in Paris to transport the 7th Division to the front. Through the night some seven hundred little Paris taxis transported the entire division.

These stumblings and improvisations have come to be called the First Battle of the Marne. Along a front of about two hundred miles there were a number of disjointed, often confused battles. The Germans were plagued by a breakdown in communications (telephones were easily knocked out and only usable over limited distances, and radio—or wireless—was still only a new gadget); the commander of one wing was not aware of the plans of the commander of his neighboring wing, and vice versa.

By September 8, it became clear to Moltke that his troops would not arrive in Paris on schedule. Worried and far from the battlefields in Luxembourg, he dispatched a member of his staff—Lieutenant Colonel Richard Hentsch, his intelligence officer—to the scene to advise Kluck and Bülow.

Hentsch assumed, perhaps because he did not fully understand the befuddled Moltke, more authority than was his due. Still, he had been empowered by the Chief of the General Staff to speed to the scene and advise the army commanders. He visited Kluck's headquarters and authorized a withdrawal of the battered First Army in order to close the gap between it and Bülow's Second Army. Kluck, who had been away at the time, did not countermand the order; he had been considering the same move—only now he had someone else to blame for it: Moltke. Hentsch moved along the front arranging a general, though organized, retreat from the Marne northward toward the Vesle River. The retreat was on.

The great Schlieffen Plan, often revised, was totally abandoned. With the Allies in not very speedy pursuit—the B.E.F. never actually exploited the opening between Kluck's and Bülow's armies—the German right wing was driven back to prepared positions along the Aisne and Vesle rivers. On this same day, September 14, Moltke was informed by the Emperor that he was relieved of his command and replaced by a younger, more vigorous commander, the Minister of War, General Erich von Falkenhayn. For a time this was kept from the German people for reasons of morale. Falkenhayn attempted to revive the Schlieffen

Joffre (second from right) near the front on the Marne; he was credited with "saving Paris" in 1914.

Plan by strengthening his right wing and attempting to break through the Allied left. This did not work, and as pressure increased on the Allied line, more troops were poured into the battle, as each side tried to outflank the other—this has been called "The Race to the Sea."

What the winner would have done once he had arrived at the sea is unknown, for all this accomplished was to establish trenches along the Aisne River to the English Channel. The Western Front was taking on its definitive, deadly form.

The Germans filled the gap between the First and Second armies by forming a new Seventh Army made up of a corps that had been freed when the Belgian fortress at Namur capitulated on September 7. Other stray units were added to the Seventh and the German line held. The line of trenches stretched eastward.

To the east—the French right and the German left—where Plan XVII had been revealed as useless, the Western Front solidified. The French had been slaughtered in the beginning as they charged into Lorraine, their officers wearing telltale white gloves—and were often the first to die. By September the Germans, too, had suffered heavily. Prince Rupprecht's Sixth Army was stopped by the hard fighting of the French First and Second armies—and the murderous guns of the forts at Epinal and Toul. The Crown Prince encountered the élan of General Maurice Sarrail's Third Army and the imperviousness of the fortresses around Verdun. Two other German armies, the Fourth and Third, floundered in the Marshes of Saint-Gond and contended with the determined *poilus* of Generals Fernand de Langle de Cary and Ferdinand Foch.

41

Another front: Bosnian troops of the Austrian Army under the command of General Potiorek, whose incompetence contributed to the events at Sarajevo.

Foch emerged as one of the French heroes of the 1914 fighting; after a severe German bayonet charge, he is reported to have declared, "My flanks are turned, my center gives way; I attack!" While undoubtedly apocryphal, the statement is in character, and by the time of the so-called Race to the Sea, Foch had been elevated from a corps commander in the Second Army to an assistant to Joffre.

Foch's mission was to co-ordinate the British and French armies in northern France. The Belgian Army finally gave up Antwerp on October 10, despite a fruitless attempt by the British to reinforce the tiny army with three ill-equipped brigades of marines provided by Winston Churchill, First Lord of the Admiralty. Churchill had arrived with the marines and offered to serve as their commander, but he was hastily ordered back home by Prime Minister Asquith.

But the tattered Belgian Army held on to a portion of their country, falling back to the Dixmud–Nieuport railway beyond the Yser River. In desperation the Belgians opened the locks on the Nieuport embankment and the sea slowly flooded the battlefields, stopping the Germans; French reinforcements that Joffre had finally sent to Nieuport destroyed those German battalions that had waded through the rising water to occupy the village of Ramscapple. The Germans withdrew and the battle flared further to the east, near the old town of Ypres.

The First Battle of Ypres (roughly October 12 to November 11) was one of the bitterest and, for Germany, one of the costliest. The focus of the battle having settled in the west, the Germans shifted troops from

42

Antwerp to join with eight reserve divisions, consisting primarily of young volunteers. They were undertrained but patriotically eager. Once in combat these youths of the new Fourth Army fought savagely—their singing could be heard over the din of battle—often overrunning British positions to wipe out entire battalions of better-trained, experienced men. Although the Germans broke through the British lines at Gheluvelt on October 31, a fierce counterattack by a handful of survivors of the 2nd Worcestershires drove them off. The Germans never got to Ypres.

A final attempt on November 11—when the Prussian Guard broke through the British line on the Menin road—was blocked and driven back. The British counterattack had employed even cooks and orderlies to stop the crack Prussian Guard. The Ypres salient remained and, drawing back, the Germans continued to pound the town with artillery.

In December, Joffre attempted to break through the German lines, first to the north of Arras, and later a larger offensive in Champagne; neither did more than add to the mounting casualty toll. The year closed with the Western Front consisting of two opposing systems of trenches, congealed in the frozen mud, farmlands, woods, hills, valleys. It extended nearly five hundred miles from the English Channel through the corner of Belgium held by the Allies, through the Artois, Picardy and Champagne regions of France, jutted around the fortresses of Verdun in Lorraine, and then stretched southward through Alsace to the Swiss border.

The fighting on the southeastern end of the front, where Joffre's Plan XVII had come to nothing, had been costly, especially to the French. Within the first two weeks, French casualties reached an appalling figure: 300,000 men killed or captured—with little or no ground gained. Historian Jack Wren has written of the plan's disastrous functioning: "The French forces made their appearance on the battlefield in the best nineteenth-century formation with smartly groomed officers, wearing white gloves, marching sixty feet in advance of their troops, who wore dusk-blue jackets and scarlet trousers. Regimental pennants and brass bands accompanied them to strike fear and terror in enemy hearts."

And then German artillery and machine guns slaughtered them; in the first month alone the French Army lost 10 per cent of its officers. Except for the killing, little else was accomplished on the French right wing (i.e., the German left) of the Western Front. Even as the Battle of the Marne began, the Germans managed an incursion, which was stopped in the so-called *Trouée de Charmes,* a gap between the French fortifications intended to channel an invading German army into a trap. Although the Germans were not annihilated, the trap worked, despite its obviousness. Although the French drained troops away from this sector to aid in the defense of Paris, by the time the Marne front raged, the

Germans and the French faced each other in Alsace-Lorraine in the stalemate that would characterize the entire Western Front by the close of 1914.

Although the front had greatly attracted the attention of the press and the world, there were lesser but no less murderous battle zones on the more widespread fronts to the east and beyond.

Austria initiated its "bright, brisk little war" to punish the Serbs for the assassinations of the Archduke and his wife by an attack across the Sava and Drina rivers from Bosnia. At the head of this ill-fated expedition was General Oskar Potiorek, who had assured the late Archduke as they drove through Sarajevo that he would "take the responsibility." His incursion into Serbia had somewhat the same disastrous results as the auto ride. He wasted some of his troops on policing duties in Bosnia and Montenegro and took the rest into Serbia, where they were met by the hardened Serbian armies fighting on their own ground and led by a wily General Radomir Putnik. By September the Austrians (actually Austro-Hungarians) were driven back across the Drina, with a loss of 50,000 men and with the Serbian armies relatively intact.

Humiliated, the Austrians made another attempt with reinforcements and better equipment early in September. They managed to hold a couple of bridgeheads and dug in. Bitter fighting in the mountains, plus a preponderance of troops and supplies, brought the Austrians into Belgrade on December 2. Putnik struck with a counteroffensive on the third, having been forced to await new supplies of ammunition. By December 16, Belgrade was reoccupied and the Austrians driven back through the bitter cold, blizzards, and rough terrain. By the end of December the Austrians had lost 100,000 men; the Serbs lost an equal number. But at the end of the year the Austrian and Serbian armies faced each other at roughly the same line where the fighting had begun in August.

About 350 miles to the north of the Austro-Serbian battlegrounds, the Austrian High Command launched yet another ill-fated drive. This one was aimed through Galicia (Austrian Poland) at Russia. The firebrand of the Austrian war party, General Franz Conrad von Hötzendorf, commanded the invading armies. He planned to strike before the Russians finished mobilizing. Conrad attacked northward toward Lublin and Kholm on August 22 and to his surprise blundered into General Nikolai Ivanov's troops—to Ivanov's surprise also. The Russian commander had expected the blow to come further south, from Lemberg (Lvov).

Conrad's left-wing armies, the First and Fourth, moved into Russian Poland, fighting indecisive, blundering battles with the Russians. The Austrian commander anticipated victory and ordered his Third Army to attack east of Lemberg, where two Russian armies were ready and waiting. Two of Ivanov's ablest tacticians, Generals Aleksei Brusilov and

44

Austrian troops preparing defenses at an altitude of more than 6,000 feet; mountain fighting was extremely difficult and required special training besides stamina.

Radko Dmitriev, struck. The stunned Austrians stopped and then fell back rapidly—leaving their dead and wounded behind. By September 3 the Third Army had been driven back to Lemberg with the Russians in full pursuit. Lemberg fell and the seemingly invincible Russian armies engulfed the fortress city of Przemysl.

Although he did not admit it, Conrad had suffered a debacle in Galicia. He and his troops would have suffered even more had not the Russians frequently revealed their positions and future plans to the Austrians by communicating by radio in clear, uncoded messages.

By September 11, Conrad ordered his armies, now mauled by the relentless Russians, to retreat. When the month ended, Austrian troops had fallen back to the Vistula River, Tarnow-Gorlice, and the Carpathian Mountains. The line was over 130 miles west of Lemberg. Conrad's military adventuring had cost him Galicia—and the cream of the Austrian Army (250,000 dead and wounded and 100,000 prisoners).

The presence of Russian troops so close to German Silesia was cause for alarm in the German camp. Unlike the Austrians, the Germans had prevailed against the Russians on the Eastern Front.

Things had gone badly for the Central Powers when the Germans and Russians first met in August. The German Eighth Army, commanded by Colonel General Max von Prittwitz, clashed with the Russian First Army (General Pavel Rennenkampf) on August 20 in the Battle of

45

Field Marshal Paul von Hindenburg, who with the aid of General Ludendorff and Lieutenant Colonel Max von Hoffmann defeated the Russians at Tannenberg and the Masurian Lakes in 1914.

Gumbinnen in East Prussia. Prittwitz, faced with the possibility of yet another Russian army (General Alexander Samsonov's Second) coming at him from the south, phoned Moltke to suggest a retreat as far back as the Vistula River. Moltke relieved Prittwitz, replacing him with the aging, retired General Paul von Hindenburg. The older man was merely a front for the real commander, General Ludendorff, the popular hero of Liège. Retained also was Prittwitz's sharp chief of operations, General Max von Hoffmann; it was Hoffmann who was aware of Rennenkampf's and Samsonov's mutual dislike. The feud would contribute to the outcome of the Battle of Tannenberg.

Rennenkampf did not exploit his victory at Gumbinnen, and Hindenburg's team of thinkers—Ludendorff and Hoffmann—elected to leave a small cavalry screen (one division) opposite the Russian First Army's twenty-four infantry divisions. If Rennenkampf noticed the mass withdrawal, he certainly did nothing about that, either. The two corps that had been withdrawn were shipped to the south to meet the threat of Samsonov's Second Army.

But Samsonov had not been blind to a German withdrawal; on August 24 a German corps commander requested permission to move his troops from the Tannenberg area to a better position on a nearby ridge. Samsonov mistook this for a general retreat by the Germans and ordered his army to begin pursuit. He did this in the Russian manner of the time —by radio in the clear. The Germans intercepted his orders. Samsonov was unaware of the approach of the two corps borrowed from Rennenkampf's front and that of another coming by rail from Königsberg and Elbing. So with Rennenkampf blithely unaware of the few German troops detaining him, Samsonov was equally unaware of the concentration of German troops descending upon him instead of, as he believed, retreating.

The German High Command had a single nagging concern: would they be able to deal with Samsonov before Rennenkampf realized the true situation? Would he be able to come to Samsonov's rescue, or rather, would he bother to, considering their personal enmity? Rennenkampf supplied the answer on August 25, when he broadcast, in the clear, his positions. It was obvious that he was too distant from the German Eighth Army approaching the hill, Tannenberg, to help Samsonov or to strike at the German rear. On the same day, Samsonov decided to ease up his "pursuit" to rest his troops.

When he resumed his advance on the twenty-sixth, Samsonov moved into a trap. In three days, a series of encounters given the name of the Battle of Tannenberg, all but destroyed Samsonov's army. He waited in vain for aid from Rennenkampf. By August 30 the battles were over for Samsonov; the Germans had taken more than 90,000 prisoners alone. But they did not take Samsonov; he disappeared into a wooded area, from which a single shot rang out, and was never seen again.

While the remnants of the Russian Second Army fled to the south, Hindenburg (i.e., Ludendorff and Hoffmann) could attend to Rennenkampf. The blow fell in the Masurian Lakes region in early September; by the ninth the Russians began a withdrawal—the troops on foot and Rennenkampf by automobile. The general did not stop until he reached Russian soil. Once again Russian casualties were high although it was no Tannenberg and thousands of prisoners were taken. The smaller Russian victories in Galicia were greatly overshadowed by the failures in East Prussia.

In Berlin there was great rejoicing and Hindenburg was hailed as a great hero. The triumphs in the east helped to counterbalance the bad news from the Marne.

There were shake-ups in Russia: Rennenkampf was accused of treason but escaped prosecution and remained at the head of what remained of the First Army. His chief and accuser (who had been in over-all command in East Prussia), General Ivan Jilinsky, was relieved of his command. The two armies he had once commanded had been torn to shreds

*The ruins of Tannenberg after the Russians were driven out
by the German Eighth Army.*

by the superior commanders of the German troops, by German guns, supplies, and mobility—the use of railroad transport to move troops to the battlefronts.

The Russian defeats at Tannenberg/Masurian Lakes did not eliminate the Imperial Russian Army from the war (although there were suggestions at the time that Russia might withdraw).

With the Russians driven out of East Prussia, Hindenburg felt he could spare troops to aid the floundering Austro-Hungarians to the south in Galicia. A new German Army was formed from units (four corps) borrowed from the Eighth Army, holding East Prussia. These troops were quickly transported south by rail to Silesia (with its valuable coal and minerals), where additional corps were added to make up the Ninth Army. Since Hindenburg was named Commander-in-Chief of German forces in the east, the Ninth Army was under the command of General August von Mackensen. This new army, which had also drawn needed men from the Western Front, moved into Silesia and took its place on the left flank of the Austrian First Army under General Viktor von Dankl.

By coincidence the Grand Duke Nicholas had been busy regrouping and reinforcing his Russian armies for a blow across the Vistula through Warsaw into Silesia and East Prussia.

The objective of the Hindenburg-Ludendorff-Hoffmann strategy was to take Warsaw by sending the Ninth Army northward, hoping to surprise the Russians entrenched along the San and Vistula rivers. The surprise was spoiled when the vanguard of the Ninth Army was spotted

48

by Russian cavalry on September 25. Both sides were by this time well informed of the plans of the enemy. Papers found on a dead German officer revealed Hindenburg's objective to the Russians, and a dead Russian soldier carried papers revealing to Hindenburg that his eighteen divisions faced no less than sixty Russian divisions. What the papers did not reveal the Russians obligingly made known by radio.

Although the news of the massing Russians gave Hindenburg pause, he followed through with the original plan. The Ninth Army moved toward Warsaw, and the Austrian First Army moved east. By October 6 the Germans approached the Vistula and the Austrians the San. On the twelfth Mackensen was within a dozen miles of Warsaw. Nicholas then unleashed his counteroffensive. Five days of savage fighting flared along the Vistula before the German left wing began to turn away from Warsaw.

The famous Russian "steamroller" took its toll, and by October 17, Mackensen decided to pull out; six days later the Ninth Army was back, after retreating some sixty miles, where it started. In its wake it left a great devastated landscape, blown bridges, burned-out villages and farms, and other random destruction.

On their portion of the front, the Austrians also bent under the Russian hordes. Accusations were exchanged: the Germans blamed their retreat on the failure of the Austrians to cross the San to strike the Russians from the south; the Austrians blamed the Germans for giving up the battle for Warsaw and for their subsequent failures.

But the Germans had not given up and were determined to stop the Russian drive into Silesia. The Ninth Army was again moved by railroad to the north and joined with units of the Eighth Army for a blow against the Russian flank. The attack, from the direction of Thorn (Torun) and Posen, opened on November 11 and smashed in a gap between the Russian First and Second armies. The opportunity for Rennenkampf to encircle the German attackers was missed and the confused fighting tumbled into a wintry December. By the sixth the Russians began to withdraw from the fortress city of Lodz and the Germans moved in. The Russian Fifth Army was ordered to assist the Second and managed to push back the German left flank and was once again inside East Prussia.

There was no clear-cut victory on the Eastern Front as the year came to an end. True, the Germans had defeated the Russians at Tannenberg; Lodz had been less spectacular. But both together spelled the end of any future decisive offensive by the Russian steamroller. Hundreds of thousands of lives had been lost in the various battles along the vast Eastern Front (it might be noted that after the loss of Lodz the most incompetent of Russian generals, Rennenkampf, was fired); with the coming of bitter winter, the Eastern Front became quiet also.

While the major battlefronts raged or bogged down, other fronts—

Helmets and trenches: British prepare for the Turkish threat to the Suez Canal. The troops are checking a trench mortar. Trenches were not new with World War I, but modern weaponry made them necessary on a miserably grand scale.

less dramatically perhaps—flickered in other parts of the world. The war took on a certain global aspect when Japan declared war on Germany on August 23, moved into the Chinese city of Kiaochow and drove out the German garrison. This, of course, helped Japan more than the Allies, although it did alleviate the threat of further Japanese-Russian misunderstandings for a while, leaving Russia to concentrate on one front. Japan eventually seized other German colonies: the Caroline, Marianas, and Marshall islands in the Pacific. These "mandates," as they were called after the war when the spoils were divided, would have to be taken back from Japan bloodily in a future war.

Germany's African colonies, fruits of the Kaiser's initial ventures in empire building, were not ignored by the French and the British. The British took Togoland before the end of August, and British-French forces occupied the Cameroons by September. German Southwest Africa took longer, but was eventually taken by the neighboring South Africans, who the Germans hoped would rise up in a sequel to the Boer War, but were greatly disappointed. By July 1915 German Southwest Africa surrendered to the Prime Minister of South Africa, General Louis Botha.

Only in East Africa did the Germans prevail, under the command of a remarkable leader, Paul von Lettow-Vorbeck, who even managed to beat the British to the punch. His troops attacked the British first in not very decisive forays, but Lettow-Vorbeck succeeded in fighting a cat-and-mouse war in the bush, jungles, rivers, and on the surface of Lake

50

Tanganyika of East Africa. The fortunes of war favored one side and then the other in an exotic setting, but Lettow-Vorbeck persisted. He harried the Allies, eluded total defeat and captivity; he was the only German general to manage this throughout the entire war.

Turkey, straddling Europe and Asia, was a secret ally of Germany when the war began. Nursing grievances against Britain and Russia, the shrunken so-called Ottoman Empire (or more popularly "the sick man of Europe") visualized an alliance with the Central Powers as an opportunity to even up matters a bit, if not to grab back some of the lost empire. Britain, suspicious of the Turks, refused to deliver two Turkish battleships then being constructed in England (although offering to return the money). Turkey protested, but the lack was made up when two German cruisers, the *Goeben* and the *Breslau,* fleeing the British in the Mediterranean, slipped into the sanctuary of Turkish ports. As a neutral, Turkey was obligated by international law to intern the vessels and crews. Instead many members of the German crews donned fezzes and were welcomed into the Turkish Navy.

Admiral Wilhelm Souchon sent his ships into the Black Sea to stir up the Russians, but without success until October 29. The Russian port of Odessa was shelled by three Turkish ships, manned partly by Germans, and by November 2, the "sick man" was officially at war with the Allies.

The German High Seas Fleet, the major challenger of the British Royal Navy. This photograph was taken from the deck of the Scharnhorst, *which was sunk in the Battle of the Falkland Islands late in 1914; so was the ship next in line,* Gneisenau.

With the Dardanelles closed to them, the Russians would suffer economically and militarily. The Allies also saw the Turks as a threat to the Suez Canal.

The British initiated small campaigns in Mesopotamia and in the vicinity of the Suez Canal, with some success. They even managed a show of British might by shelling the Turkish Dardanelles forts from the sea. But the Turkish Minister of War, Enver Pasha, concentrated his attentions and his Third Army on the Russian frontier. The fighting in the freezing, mountainous country of the Caucasus was almost as brutal as the weather and the terrain. In November Enver commanded about 150,000 ill-equipped troops, which he led against the smaller Russian Seventh Army (which was properly clothed for the cold) on December 17. Although initially successful, the Turks by the turn of the new year suffered a heavy defeat. Those hapless Turks who were not killed by the Russians froze to death by the thousands—or were captured, even deserted. An entire corps simply gave up; between 30,000 and 50,000 frozen Turks were found in the frigid mountain passes. Only 12,000 troops retreated back to Turkey.

Only the sea provided vaster settings for battle than the Eastern Front. Most of the major confrontations between the two major naval powers, Britain and Germany, occurred in the Atlantic. The German cruiser *Emden* severely interfered with shipping in the Indian Ocean until, in November, it was destroyed by an Australian cruiser, *Sydney*.

The Germans were reluctant to risk their High Seas Fleet in an all-out naval battle with the British Grand Fleet, which was the more powerful of the two. Initially it was hoped that by pecking away at the Grand Fleet the High Seas Fleet could eventually challenge the British as near equals. The Grand Fleet had played an important role in the seizure of Germany's African colonies and could interfere with the shipping of supplies in the North Sea and the Mediterranean. This prompted the "father of the German Navy," Admiral Alfred von Tirpitz, to rely upon his fleet of submarines to deal with the Royal Navy as well as Allied and neutral shipping.

The British enjoyed not only superiority—the Royal Navy had two dozen big-gunned "dreadnoughts" to Germany's thirteen—but also a traditional understanding of sea power the Germans lacked. A characteristic British raid occurred at the end of August, when the dashing Vice Admiral Sir David Beatty led a squadron of battle cruisers out of the fog to attack German ships based at Heligoland, a small island in the North Sea and a major German naval base. Beatty's ships swooped in and out without losing a ship and left three sunken German cruisers and a destroyer.

52

HMS Inflexible, *a battle cruiser that took part in the Battle of the Falkland Islands in the South Atlantic.*

It was a clear-cut victory for the British, although the German Navy began its work in earnest the following month. In September the submarine U-9 sank three British cruisers off the coast of Holland, practically in British waters. These waters around and leading into the British Isles were mined by the Germans and in October the battleship *Audacious* struck a mine off the Irish coast and sank. A few days later, on the twentieth, the submarine U-17 accounted for the first merchant vessel, the British *Glitra,* the opening blow in the battle of submarine vs. unarmed supply ship.

A more typical sea battle took place off Coronel, Chile, on November 1. Under Admiral Count Maximilian von Spee, the Asian Squadron headed homeward (leaving the *Emden* to harry British shipping until it was finally destroyed) via the South Atlantic. The British were anxious to intercept Spee, whose unit numbered a couple of armored cruisers. When the British force, under Rear Admiral Sir Christopher Cradock, confronted the Germans, Spee commanded four cruisers two of which had joined him along the way; Cradock had mustered an old battleship, two armored cruisers, and a light cruiser. The battle was brief and ferocious; Cradock went down with his burning ship, *Good Hope;* the cruiser *Monmouth,* also blazing, soon followed. All hands on both ships 1,654 men—were lost. Two British ships, *Otranto* and *Glasgow* (which had taken several hits), fled the scene.

53

Stunned by the disaster, the Admiralty detached two battle cruisers from the Grand Fleet, *Invincible* and *Inflexible,* and ordered them to the South Atlantic. These were joined by others, under the command of Vice Admiral Sir F. Doveton Sturdee. By December 7 the British squadron was in and around Port Stanley in the Falkland Islands for refueling. They had yet to spot Spee and his ships.

Spee meanwhile had rounded Cape Horn and had decided, against the advice of his senior officers, to shell the British ports in the Falklands. The British ships were not ready to give battle because of the refueling and boiler inspection when the approach of Spee was noted. Instead of shelling the ships at anchor in the ports, Spee decided instead to get away; he wanted no confrontation with British warships.

As soon as he was ready Sturdee ordered his ships in pursuit. The German turnabout had positioned their ships about twelve miles ahead of the British ships, which had the advantage of speed. By one o'clock in the afternoon of December 8, the Battle of the Falkland Islands began: Coronel was avenged, with interest. Before the day ended six German ships had been destroyed, including the great armored cruisers *Scharnhorst* and *Gneisenau.* Even two supply ships were destroyed in the mopping up. Of the seven German ships under Spee's command, one—the cruiser *Dresden*—managed to escape (it was caught the following March by the British; the captain put up a white flag and then blew up his vessel).

The Falkland Islands battle was a German disaster—the loss of six ships and more than 2,000 seamen, including Spee and his two sons. Two hundred survivors were rescued from the freezing Atlantic by the British, whose losses were slight, thanks to their ships' armor and longer-ranged guns.

With the Atlantic and Pacific oceans cleared of German warships, the Royal Navy could concentrate on keeping the rest of the German Navy bottled up in the North Sea. But the High Seas Fleet was not totally finished, as was proved on December 16, when several German cruisers appeared out of the mists off northeast England and shelled the coastal towns of Scarborough, Whitby, and Hartlepool. Before the Royal Navy could do anything about it, the German ships slipped away, leaving behind nearly 500 civilians dead in the three towns.

War upon civilians was an entirely new concept and shook the English (although the full truth of the extent of the casualties and damage was kept out of the news). The popular music hall song, "Oh, What a Lovely War!" took on a hollow ring at home and on the battlefronts as 1914 ended in a staggering stalemate. Lord Kitchener himself provided the ironic quote of the year upon viewing the carnage of First Ypres. "This isn't war!" he exclaimed.

He was wrong.

*The Kaiser orders mobilization of the German
Army; below his signature is that of
the Chancellor, Theobald von Bethmann-Hollweg.*

German cavalry leaving Berlin for Paris as their countrymen and women cheer them on.

French soldiers passing through a village; in the vanguard, mounted scouts on horses and bicycles.

Mobilization begins in France.

Helmuth von Moltke, the first, a respected military planner and the first Chief of the German General Staff. His was an honored name among Prussian military thinkers.

German Information Center

British recruits, with a band in the lead, marching to Waterloo Station and shipment to military training camps.

Imperial War Museum

*Britain comes to the aid of an ally. The first (of thirty-seven)
Royal Flying Corps B.E.2s that crossed the Channel and landed
in France, August 12, 1914. The pilot, under the nose of the plane,
is Lieutenant H. D. Harvey-Kelly of No. 2 Squadron.*

*Sir John French, commander of the British
Expeditionary Force in France, 1914.*

British cavalrymen of the 11th Hussars resting after the retreat from Mons.

Belgian troops behind a makeshift barricade await the Germans on the outskirts of Louvain—the retreat of Antwerp has begun.

Modern means of transportation. Paul L. Maze an interpreter, astride his motorcycle. Since most British officers could not speak French, interpreters were extremely important.

Members of Kluck's First Army moving through Brussels.

Belgian peasants suspected of passing information to the French have been sentenced by a German court-martial to be shot. Ruthless German treatment of Belgian civilians led to often untrue stories of German atrocities.

German artillery moving into position. The troops are burdened with full field equipment and wearing the old Pickelhaube helmet.

Germans on the march through a Belgian village during the Ypres offensive.

ORDRE
A LA POPULATION LIÉGEOISE

La population d'Andenne, après avoir témoigné des
entions pacifiques à l'égard de nos troupes, les a atta-
ées de la façon la plus traîtresse. Avec mon autorisation,
énéral qui commandait ces troupes a mis la ville en
ndres et a fait fusiller 110 personnes.
le porte ce fait à la connaissance de la Ville de Liége
ir que ses habitants sachent à quel sort ils peuvent
tendre s'ils prennent une attitude semblable.

41 31

Liége, le 22 Août 1914.

Général von BULOW.

Commander of the German Second Army, General Karl von Bülow warns the people of Liège that civilian interference with the advance of the Germans will be ruthlessly punished. As an example he invokes the village of Andenne, where he authorized the execution of 110 civilians. Such slaughter led to the Belgian atrocity stories.

German troops resting in a battle-damaged Belgian town.

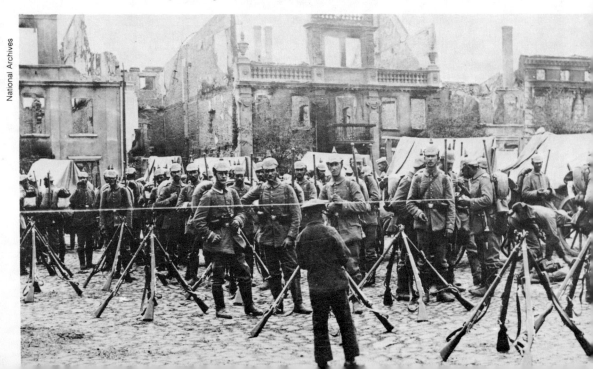

General Joseph Gallieni, Military
Governor of Paris, during the First
Battle of the Marne.

One of Gallieni's famous Taxis of the Marne, which were used to bring
reinforcements to the front to stop the German advance on Paris.

General Erich von Falkenhayn,
German Minister of War when
war was declared, and later Chief
of Staff when Moltke was relieved.

British soldiers wearing German booty, after a German withdrawal from the Marne.

A British Rolls-Royce armored car on the Menin road, which led to Ypres, just prior to the battle.

British infantrymen during the First Battle of Ypres, taking shelter from shrapnel.

The Cloth Hall, Ypres, before German shells began falling into the city.

British 2nd Scots Guards passing through a Belgian village in the race to the sea.

Kitchener calls on his countrymen to take up arms. The original poster, by artist Alfred Leete, appeared first as a cover of the London Opinion *in September 1914.*

An Austrian machine-gun emplacement on the Austrian-Serbian frontier.

*Max von Hoffmann (center), chief architect of the German victories in Russia.
To his left, Prince Leopold of Bavaria, who introduced the use of
poison gas against the Russians in 1914.*

German troops being transported to East Prussia on the Eastern Front, August 1914. The German utilization of international rail lines contributed greatly to many of the early German victories.

German East Africa and the good life. Count Paul Lettow-Vorbeck (second from right), who took command of the German forces in East Africa and managed to elude the Allies throughout the war.

War at sea: HMS Audacious *sinking after hitting a mine off the coast of Ulster; rescue craft move in to remove the survivors. The loss of the* Audacious *was kept secret until the war was over; the British High Command believed its sinking would have had a poor effect on morale.*

German seamen from the sunken Gneisenau *awaiting rescue by the British. The* Inflexible *is in the background.*

*Horatio Herbert Kitchener, British Secretary of State for War, 1914,
was credited with creating a first-rate professional British Army.*

American volunteers fighting in France. They served with the French Foreign Legion (which did not require an oath of allegiance, which would have lost the volunteers their American citizenship). In the foreground: Kiffin Rockwell, who eventually transferred to the Lafayette Escadrille.

1915

"Keep the Homes Fires Burning"

THE WAR that everyone had expected would be over before winter dragged on. To seasoned—if not necessarily experienced—soldiers it was inexplicable. What kind of war was this?

It made good sense to those who believed in the offensive: to hurl great bodies of men against other great bodies in defensive positions and take them. The greater number of bodies, it followed, won. The French High Command was especially incensed over the German presence on French soil. This preoccupied Joffre, despite the victory—if such it was —on the Marne. He planned a spring offensive and expected to be at the Rhine by autumn. The Western Front battle would decide the issue, Joffre maintained while choosing to ignore the trenches, mud, and machine guns. As 1915 dawned nearly two million Germans faced about three million Allied soldiers across those muddy, barbed-wired trenches along the Western Front.

The Central Powers were of two strategic minds. Falkenhayn, who had superseded Moltke, agreed with his French counterpart, Joffre: the war would be decided in the west. But he was opposed by the Hindenburg-Ludendorff team in the east. Their stars shone so brightly that they could afford to defy their superior. Falkenhayn hoped for a breakthrough on the Western Front, and Hindenburg-Ludendorff hoped for the elimination of Russia on the Eastern Front. The dispute, finally, had to be decided by the Kaiser, who authorized, to Falkenhayn's discomfort, reinforcements for the Eastern Front; four recently mobilized corps were sent to bolster the Germans and Austro-Hungarians facing the Russian armies.

Ludendorff planned a two-pronged push, the Germans out of East Prussia and the Austrians through Galicia. As fate had it, Conrad's push was met by an even larger Russian offensive and the Austrian half of the

73

Theater of war: No Man's Land at night. Flares illuminated the terrain to immobilize marauding parties from both sides. Barbed wire made passage through No Man's Land very difficult.

prong was stopped and steamrolled back; by March 23 the Russians took the fortress of Przemysl and more than 100,000 prisoners and their weapons. The Russians also commanded passes through the Carpathians which led into the Hungarian plains.

The northern pincer, under the Hindenburg-Ludendorff command, was successful in the second battle of the Masurian Lakes. In the east a new Tenth Army, commanded by General Hermann von Eichhorn, was formed with reinforcements from the Kaiser. The major objective was to wipe out the Russian Tenth Army. The attack began with a diversionary move by one corps of the German Ninth Army as it moved in to cover the flank of the German Eighth, facing Warsaw. For the first time, on January 31, 1915, poison gas was used in warfare. The Germans fired thousands of shells filled with chlorine (tear gas) near the Polish town

Russian machine guns in German hands after the victories in East Prussia.

of Bolimov—to no effect. A combination of cold weather and inexperience canceled out the new weapon so far as the Germans were concerned. The Russians evinced little curiosity in the strange clouds on the battlefield; nor did the Russian High Command inform their allies in the west of the appearance of a new German weapon. It was a lesson they would have to learn painfully themselves in the near future.

The battle proper was launched during a furious snowstorm in early February and raged for weeks, at times in waist-deep snow. The Russian Tenth Army was virtually annihilated (about 200,000 men, half of them taken prisoner), although the plan to encircle and totally destroy it was not carried through. Even Falkenhayn realized that the Austrians needed bolstering and that the sooner the Russians were eliminated from the war the sooner he could give his full attention to the Western Front.

Imperial War Museum

*The real war: a French listening post
near the lines on the Western Front.*

Falkenhayn went further: he detached the newly formed Eleventh Army from the Western Front and sent it east.

Under the command of General August von Mackensen the army was placed in the Gorlice-Tarnow area, just north of the Carpathians; he also commanded the Austrian Fourth Army. By the beginning of May some fourteen German-Austrian divisions faced six Russian divisions, which were not only outnumbered but ill-equipped—some soldiers did not even have guns, and shoes and ammunition were lacking for those who had guns. Mackensen's former command, the Ninth Army, was turned over to a veteran, Prince Leopold of Bavaria, further north in the area of Lodz and was pointed at Warsaw and the Vistula River.

77

In East Prussia, Hindenburg had slipped a little in his eastern command because of the presence of Falkenhayn, who had moved his headquarters to the Eastern Front to oversee what he hoped would be the conclusive battle there. He could also keep an eye on Hindenburg and Ludendorff, who continued to criticize him in the hearing of the Kaiser. Hindenburg was assigned the job of striking an opening diversionary blow into Lithuania, screening the major moves in Poland and Galicia. Leopold's attack began on May 2 with a gas attack which, though successful, was not exploited by the Germans, who thought it had failed. Another gas attack into the wind did more harm to German troops than to Russian. But the attack pushed on.

The major blow began when nearly a thousand German guns began hammering the Russians along the front from the Vistula to the Carpathians. Within two days, on May 4, the Russian Fourth Army crumbled and Mackensen's troops broke through. In two weeks the Germans had advanced about eighty miles to the San River. By June the

Major General Hans von Beseler, who occupied Antwerp in 1914 and became Military Governor of Warsaw after the Russians were driven out in 1915.

fortress Przemysl again changed hands and was back under the control of the Central Powers. Even the southern end of the line, under the command of Conrad, began pushing the Russians away from the Carpathians into the Ukraine. Russian prisoners were taken by the thousands.

But the Central Powers had some disquieting concerns by June: Italy had come into the war on the side of the Allies, creating yet another battleground on the Austro-Hungarian border. This was especially galling because Italy had been, on paper at least, tied to Germany by the Triple Alliance. Yet another distracting event was the landing of Allied troops at Gallipoli in the Dardanelles, a move initiated to help the Russians. It helped no one and proved to be a British disaster—although Falkenhayn and company were not aware of this in June 1915. Conrad proposed yet another distraction by suggesting that some divisions be detached from Galicia and sent to the Gorizia region of northeastern Italy to smite the Italians along the Isonzo River.

But the Kaiser prevailed and the offensive proceeded deeper into Russia despite Falkenhayn's anxiety about the Western Front.

Austrian and German armies occupied Lemberg (Lvov) on June 22, pushing the Russians to the Bug River. The advance was not one continuous flow, for as the Austro-German armies stopped to consolidate and count the thousands of Russian prisoners, Falkenhayn suggested letting it go there and to get on with the war in the west. Thus the advance started and stopped along the various sections of the battle line. This enabled the Russians, under the Grand Duke Nicholas, to escape total encirclement, although the losses in men and ground were heavy.

The Russians were driven out of Poland and Warsaw was taken by August 5; the roads were choked by fleeing civilians and soldiers. At the northern end of the battle line Hindenburg's troops captured Vilna in Lithuania and approached Riga. By the end of September, when the time came to consider digging in for the winter, the German-Austrian line, now deep inside Russia, ran from the Baltic, just short of Riga, through the Pripet Marshes to Czernowitz near the Rumanian frontier. Though victorious, the Central Powers had fallen short of their objective: the complete destruction of the Russian armies.

The Grand Duke had somehow managed to salvage his forces despite appalling supply shortages (soldiers were in good supply, however). Even so, the Czar's uncle was relieved of his command after the September losses. Influenced by the Czarina (who, in turn, was under the sway of the so-called "Mad Monk," Rasputin), the Czar turned away his able uncle and provided the Germans with the one element they needed for a victory in Russia: the Czar himself took over the "supreme command of all forces of the sea and land armies . . ." He concluded, "We shall not

79

General August von Mackensen (left) with aide on morning ride. Mackensen was selected to deal with the Serbs once and for all.

dishonor the Russian land." Not a military thinker, detached from that Russian land he promised to defend, Czar Nicholas set the scene for the disaster the Germans had failed to achieve.

With the Eastern Front stabilized for the winter, the Germans felt free to turn to the Balkan problem, which proved to be too much for Conrad's Austrian armies. In 1914 three attempts to invade Serbia had been repulsed. The time had come to deal with the Serbs.

In recognition of his performance on the Eastern Front, Mackensen was promoted to field marshal and placed in command of three armies, his own Eleventh, shifted from the Russian front to the Danube, the Austrian Third, and the Bulgarian First. The Bulgarian Government had elected to join the Central Powers secretly in September, a decision based upon a grudge against Serbia dating from the Second Balkan War, of 1913, and upon the belief in 1915 that the Allies were losing the war. Although the Serbian Army, commanded by General Radomir Putnik, had held off the Austrian armies for more than a year, its numbers had been decimated to about 200,000. The Bulgarian Army alone could muster more than 300,000 men and the combined Austro-German armies under Mackensen's command numbered 250,000.

Mackensen's men moved southward on October 6, crossing the Danube, driving the outnumbered Serbs before them; Belgrade fell on the ninth. Two days later, the Bulgarian armies began moving from the east (the First Army) and the south (the Second Army under the command of the Bulgarian king, Ferdinand—yet another relative of the Kaiser). The Serbian Army, severely pummeled from the north and east, fell back, fighting. The retreat was fought savagely over mountainous country to Albania and the Adriatic Sea. The remnants of the beaten army—about 140,000 men—"dirty skeletons in rags," starving and emaciated, reached the sea. The survivors were evacuated to Corfu by the Allies.

The Allies had made a tardy, fruitless attempt to aid Serbia just days before Mackensen struck. An "Army of the Orient" was organized under French General Maurice Sarrail (whom Joffre wished out of his hair) and shipped to Greece, which was a neutral but whose Premier, Eleutherios Venizelos, favored the Allies. Sarrail's troops began landing at Salonika on October 3 and actually pushed northward to Krivolak, a distance of about sixty-five miles, and clashed with the Bulgarian Second Army, which had already cut the rail line connecting Greece with Serbia.

It was then impossible—if it ever had been possible—for the French relief force to go to the aid of Putnik's battered Serbian Army. With the Bulgars holding fast and the Greeks still not at war with the Central Powers, Sarrail could only return to Salonika, where he would remain for the duration, accomplishing practically nothing. He should not have stayed, but he could not leave. So he established defensive positions around Salonika. Those entrapped there called it the "Bird Cage"; the Germans, with much truth, called it the Allies' largest concentration camp.

A related, though more disastrous, venture into what has been called "eccentric strategy" was attempted by the British in the Dardanelles. Its most powerful champion was the First Lord of the Admiralty, Winston Churchill, who saw such a move as a worthy alternative to "sending our armies to chew barbed wires in Flanders." On paper, seizing the Dardanelles was promising: it would secure a supply line to Russia, it might knock Turkey out of the war, it would help Serbia and, of course, draw the attention of the Central Powers to yet another front.

Beyond this grand strategy there was really no plan. Another advocate of the idea was the First Sea Lord, Admiral John Fisher, who at age seventy-four had been called from retirement to replace Prince Louis of Battenberg, who, because of his German background and a bitter anti-German sentiment in England, resigned as First Sea Lord (later the family name was changed to Mountbatten).

The First Sea Lord visualized the taking of the Dardanelles by sea power alone and assigned the task to Vice Admiral Sir Sackville Carden, commanding in the Mediterranean. Carden agreed that it could be done (Churchill did not, feeling that land forces would be needed, but went along). The Dardanelles forms a narrow channel that connects the Mediterranean and the Aegean seas with the Sea of Marmara and eventually

81

The Iron Gate on the Danube, the Austrian-Serbian frontier. Mountainous country and river crossings made this battlefront a tough one, especially in the winter.

with the Black Sea. It was believed that if a goodly number of British battleships forced their way into the channel (with the Gallipoli Peninsula to the north and Turkey proper to the south), elude the minefields, and destroy the heavy guns emplaced along both sides, the battle would be won. What might happen after that, no one appears to have considered. But as history would have it, that question never arose.

Carden began the operation on February 19 with a fleet of eighteen British warships, plus four French battleships and auxiliary ships. Bombardment of the outer forts drove the Turks from their positions, and landing parties of marines and sailors went ashore to demolish the guns. Very bad weather interfered with further shellings, and British minesweepers, manned by civilian fishermen, bogged down when faced with shellfire in the Narrows. The pressure and uncertainties broke Carden, who was replaced by Rear Admiral Sir John de Robeck in mid-March.

On March 18 the assault resumed and de Robeck nearly succeeded. By early afternoon the British guns had all but silenced the Turkish guns on shore, when a French battleship struck an unsuspected minefield and sank within minutes, taking most of the crew. Later two British battle-

82

ships struck the same field and floundered; yet another hit a mine and came under revived Turkish gunfire from the shore. De Robeck got out, not knowing how close he had been to victory. He was willing to leave the taking of the Dardanelles to the Army.

The problem fell to an observer of the naval battle, General Sir Ian Hamilton, who had been sent out by his commander, Lord Kitchener. They both agreed: the Dardanelles could not be taken by the fleet alone. Hamilton's expeditionary force, hastily thrown together, prepared to storm the shores of Gallipoli. Meanwhile, expecting this, the Turks brought up reinforcements, the Turkish Fifth Army under Mustafa Kemal, who was advised by the German General Otto Liman von Sanders. Between the time de Robeck called off the battle in the Dardanelles and Hamilton was ready to direct amphibious landings, the Turks had six weeks to prepare for them.

What was to become an epic in futility began with some success on April 25. Two limited beachheads were established at Cape Helles and Ari Burnu at the southern tip of the peninsula. The last, to the west of Helles, was occupied by the Australian and New Zealand Corps, thus

Sir Ian Hamilton (sixth from left) and staff at Gallipoli.   83

General Otto Liman von Sanders, German adviser to the Turks and thorn-in-the-side to the Allies in the Dardanelles.

the acronym Anzac. The British 29th Division landed at five spots about fifteen miles to the east. Other British and French units made diversionary moves but made no permanent landings. The British feint in the Gulf of Saros worked and the Turks rushed their reserves to Bulair in the north, leaving only a single division to deal with the Anzac-British forces that had landed on the Gallipoli Peninsula.

Hamilton, lacking intelligence about the enemy, could not co-ordinate his attacks against them. (It was said he arrived on the scene with only an inaccurate map, an outdated handbook on the Turkish Army, and a report on the Dardanelles forts.) Hamilton, who was reputed to be the British Army's most gifted writer, was not a well-informed tactician when the landings were made. Unco-ordinated, landings of the two beachheads bogged down by the second day; one commander even considered abandoning one of them, which was suffering heavily under Turkish counterattacks. Hamilton's suggestion—it was hardly an order—was, "Now you have only to dig, dig, dig until you are safe."

Indian troops boarding ship in Alexandria, Egypt, for Gallipoli.

British troops of the 42nd Division, en route to the beaches of Gallipoli.

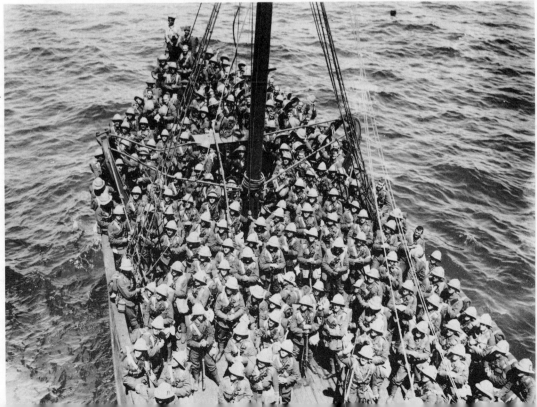

Nothing wasted—and nothing gained. Salvaging scrap for bombs, Gallipoli.

Trench warfare had arrived at Gallipoli and, like the variant on the Western Front, was the pathway to stalemate. The fact was: the British, Anzacs, and French were pinned down and were harried by the Turks, who occupied higher ground with a good view of the beaches. The British, with their backs to the sea, held their own. Attempts to break out failed, resulting only in severe Allied casualties. Neither side gained much in the skirmishing: the Turks could not push the Allies into the sea and the Allies could not force the Turks inland far enough to gain the advantages of the higher ground.

Gallipoli festered. Malaria and dysentery afflicted the British and French in the warmer months as time dragged on without much change in the battle lines. In the waters off the beaches the enemy took its toll; the British battleship *Goliath* was sunk on May 13 by a Turkish destroyer that had slipped into Morto Bay, off Cape Helles. Later in the month German U-boats accounted for two more battleships, the *Triumph* and *Majestic*. The Royal Navy looked upon the Gallipoli campaign with misgiving; Lord Fisher threatened to resign (which he eventually did) if the *Queen Elizabeth* was not taken out of harm's way (the *Elizabeth* was one of the newest battleships armed with fifteen-inch guns).

Grudgingly, additional divisions were pilfered from the Western Front and sent to Hamilton. In August he tried to force a landing at Suvla

Bay, in conjunction with a surprise attack by the Anzacs out of what was now named Anzac Cove; both to a degree succeeded. But at Anzac the objective, the ridge commanding the beach, was not reached because one column marched into itself, got confused, and spent time straightening itself out—by which time the Turks had recovered and were ready. Another column stopped just short of the objective and took time out for breakfast—when that was finished the ridge literally "bristled," as one observer put it, with Turkish rifles.

At Suvla 20,000 men were safely put ashore, hoping to outflank the Turks engaged at Anzac. Their commander, General Sir Frederick Stopford, arrived upon the scene, was pleased with the way things seemed to be going, and went to bed. A day passed before Hamilton realized the situation and courteously—as was his manner—suggested that something should be done. It was too late, for the Turkish reserves, spurred by a tough Sanders, had rushed to the scene.

Carnage at Cape Helles. Although the Allies gained a foothold, the Turks, commanded by Liman von Sanders, confined them to the beaches.

With the promise of autumn's wet weather and nothing gained over so long a period of time, the implication of withdrawal was impressed on the home front, at least among the military who saw the situation realistically. To some, of course, to evacuate (retreat) was unthinkable and they visualized an additional 50,000 casualties if that happened.

But there was little enthusiasm for the battle for Gallipoli, though Hamilton continued to have faith—even after two British and one French division were taken from him in September to be sent to the Bird Cage at Salonika. In October, Hamilton was called home and replaced by General Sir Charles Monro. Visiting the beaches, Monro had one simple suggestion: get out. But it was not until Kitchener visited the scene himself (and experienced pressure on him when he returned to London) that Monro's decision was accepted. The evacuation began on December 18, but not before the winter rains and cold drowned or froze more than 200 men in their trenches. (The evacuation was completed by January 9, 1916, without a loss.) Of the nearly 490,000 Allied troops siphoned off to Gallipoli, more than 250,000 made the casualty lists (killed, wounded, missing, or ill); of the million Turks about the same number of casualties were suffered.

Much had been ventured and little gained; the Gallipoli campaign had failed, ironically, at the moment when the Turks were all but exhausted. All that had been accomplished was to draw the attention of Falkenhayn away from the Western Front and thus spare French and Joffre his full attention as he might have wished. The British and French leaders had never approved of wasting their cannon fodder on the Dardanelles.

Denied by Gallipoli the march to Constantinople, the British were attracted to yet another fabled city, Baghdad, in Mesopotamia, where they also fought the Turks. British forces occupied Basra in November 1914—the object being to protect the Persian oil fields. In April 1915 the Turks' attempt to recover Basra failed and the British commander, General John Nixon, decided that the time had come to assure the security of his command and to move northward along the Tigris and Euphrates valleys. The major job was handed over to Major General Charles Townshend, commanding the 6th Indian Division. In June, Townshend led his troops north, reaching 'Amara on the Tigris and An Nasiriya on the Euphrates; the road to the oil fields was secure. But the victory produced a desire for more and Townshend again moved forward in September, defeating the Turks at Kut-el-Amara, pushing them further inland with his cavalry in pursuit. Baghdad lay enticingly within reach; Nixon, after checking with London, ordered Townshend forward.

The Turks, though low on morale, were greater in numbers (about double) and in position at Ctesiphon. On November 22 Townshend attacked head-on. The Turks, shaken and fearing a flanking movement as

Lord Kitchener himself visits a front-line trench at Gallipoli with Anzac commander Sir William Birdwood. It was enough to convince Kitchener that to continue the military operations on Gallipoli was pointless.

rumors had it, were ordered to retreat. The battle raged for several days and Townshend, disheartened by his own casualties, ordered his troops to fall back to Kut-el-Amara on November 26. The Turks, recovering first, began the pursuit southward; by December 7, Townshend and his small army of 8,000 Anglo-Indians were imprisoned inside Kut, surrounded by Turks, and awaiting reinforcements that never came. Under the generalship of General Kolmar von der Goltz, the Turks repulsed attempts to relieve the troops in Kut. When the year ended, there was no hope for Townshend (not even a vain attempt by the British to bribe the Turks).

"Mespot," as it came to be called, was yet another failure on the far-flung colonial fronts; the failure at Gallipoli had even improved Turkish morale and released troops to fight in Mesopotamia. Ultimately the Allies lost 40,000 men in fruitless battle. On April 29, 1916, Townshend, after more than four months of waiting for help, with his men ill and dying of malaria, surrendered to the Turks.

On yet another colonial front, the British were shaken by the remarkable feat of Ahmed Djemal Pasha, the Turkish commander in Syria. Crossing more than a hundred miles of desert, Djemal Pasha brought nearly 20,000 troops within striking distance of the Suez Canal; a small number had even crossed into Egypt. They were driven back as much by overextended supply lines as by the British. The result was that the number of Allied troops sent to Egypt increased after that February scare.

89

The colonial fronts in the Middle East and Africa, a nonproductive sideshow on the Austro-Italian border, and especially that eyesore, the Eastern Front, assailed the sensibilities of those warriors who believed that the outcome of the war must be decided on the Western Front. Scattered markings all over the map were decidedly untidy. During 1915 little would change the lines on their front.

Commanders of the Western Front—Allied as well as those of the Central Powers—fought to keep their divisions and reserves from being frittered away on sideshows. They competed for men, for supplies, and for the attention of the home front. The British had lost heavily in 1914, decimating one of the best professional armies in the world. Recruitment took on a shrill tone (the thought of conscripting an army of amateurs was unthinkable to the British High Command). The poster showing Kitchener, mustache bristling, eyes arresting the viewer, and finger pointing, indicating to Britons that they were sorely wanted, appeared widely in 1915.

Recruiting posters appealed to "The Young Women of London: Is your 'Best Boy' wearing Khaki? If not, don't *YOU THINK* he should be? If he does not think that you and your country are worth fighting for —do you think he is WORTHY of you?" While, in truth, the recruiting drive was not as successful as expected, it turned up enough men for the man-devouring Western Front for the year.

In France, although there was yet no Supreme Commander, the bulky Joffre dominated the scene. The British, though self-conscious over the comparatively small contribution—37 divisions to France's 107—of their professional army, deferred. This was part of Kitchener's plan, for he was looking forward to the day of a Supreme Allied Commander, a job for which he felt eminently qualified. (Interestingly, he was the only British leader who was fluent in French; Sir John French and Sir Douglas Haig had to depend on interpreters—a situation frequently liable to misunderstanding.)

Heartened by the "victory" on the Marne, Joffre wished to press on: offensive was the single solution. The presence of the German Army deep inside France was disturbing, and there was an unsightly bulge that ran from the North Sea to, roughly, Verdun. One salient, in the area of Compiègne and Soissons, was a mere fifty miles from Paris.

In mid-February, Joffre ordered a strike against the right flank of the repugnant bulge in Champagne; the battle petered out a month later, resulting in numerous dead, German and French. Joffre had exchanged 50,000 Frenchmen for 500 yards of churned-up French earth. The British were next. On the western flank of the bulge Haig's First Army, after an elaborate artillery preparation along a reasonably limited 3,500-yard front, broke through a narrow gap in the German lines at Neuve-Chapelle. Then "an astonishing paralysis crept over the whole move-

Daddy, what did *YOU* do in the Great War?

Recruiting poster, 1915. One question is worth a thousand speeches.

Come Now

Your arms uniform and accoutrements are ready waiting for you

Lord Kitchener at Guildhall July 1915

Be honest with yourself

Kitchener attempts to rebuild the army that had been all but destroyed in France in 1914–15.

ment," the British Official History has noted. About 10,000 men "lay, sat or stood uselessly in the mud" awaiting orders which came hours later at dusk, by which time the Germans had brought up reserves. Three days later the British still held a shattered Neuve-Chapelle and some 1,500 prisoners at a cost of 13,000 casualties and the expenditure of copious amounts of shells. Nothing really had been gained.

The French followed in April when an attempt was made to reduce the Saint-Mihiel salient (the battle of the Woëvre), east of Verdun. The results: minimal, and the salient would remain until 1918. This battle ran out of steam by April 24; by this date the Allies had other preoccupations.

For the first time on the Western Front the Germans released poison gas (this was to obscure the withdrawal of troops for duty on the Eastern Front). There was then no plan for a German breakthrough as the Germans began shelling the Ypres salient in Flanders in the morning of April 22. Taken by surprise when the greenish mist began wafting over the French positions, the French 45th Reserve Regiment abandoned their trenches and ran, leaving a four-mile gap in the line, exposing the First Canadian Division's flank.

Unaware of their initial success and without reserves, the Germans failed to exploit the break in the line. By morning the gap had been filled by British reserves (Canadian, English, and Indian) and the Second Battle of Ypres continued until May 25, with the salient slightly reduced. Allied losses amounted to 60,000 and the Germans' to about 35,000.

Foch decided to take back what had been lost by counterattack, despite the exhaustion of the troops around Ypres. His own infantry remained in their trenches at zero hour. When astute General Sir Smith-Dorrien objected to the fruitless but costly offensives, Sir John French relieved him of his command of the Second Army. Within days French himself ordered a withdrawal that only slightly shrank the salient, which

No place like home: elaborate British entrenchments near Ypres, Belgium.

A village near Arras, one of the many destroyed during the 1915 fighting in the area between Ypres and Arras; little ground was gained and casualties were high.

was of no strategic importance—just another unseemly bump in the line. In the view of historian Liddell Hart, for the next two years the British who held it "would merely serve as an easy target for German artillery practice."

A co-ordinated attack was attempted in May, both the British and French opening the battle on the ninth. Hundreds of heavy guns and nearly a thousand smaller French artillery pieces shattered the peace of a bright May morning; surprise was not the object and the guns bombarded the German lines for six days. In the northern part of the sector the British, jumping off in the area of Festubert, hoped to reach Aubers Ridge and to the south the French, starting from Souchez, had Vimy Ridge as an objective.

The British, who did not have the great numbers of guns and were also short of ammunition, enjoyed only a half hour's artillery barrage in their sector before going over the top. The well-dug-in Germans were ready, and although the British took some ground, they lost men wholesale to machine guns. On one day as high as 11,500 men were killed, wounded, or missing, though Sir John French did officially announce that his First Army (under Haig) had taken the "entire [German] first line systems of trenches . . ." True, except that the Germans had merely moved back to their secondary trenches from which they continued to slaughter the British as they dutifully went over the top. The attack sput-

94

tered out within days and even someone at Haig's headquarters admitted that it "had failed badly." Sir John French was ready with an excuse: a shortage of munitions. The home front had failed the British Expeditionary Force, not its High Command.

For a time, to their surprise, the French fared better in Artois; XXXIII Corps actually penetrated the German lines two miles and produced another war hero, General Philippe Pétain. But when the French reserves attempted to squeeze through the gap, they too ran into vicious machine-gun fire deeper inside the German trench system. As in the north, the ground taken could be measured in yards and French casualties in the thousands. The battle that Joffre had announced would mark "the beginning of the end" (he even predicted the war's end within three months if the attack were as successful as he expected), was a disaster for France. More than 100,000 casualties in fruitless local offensives led to a public outcry and criticism of Joffre. The high British casualties prompted serious questions of Sir John, but he had his "ammunition shortage" story ready.

Joffre smiled enigmatically and replied, *"Je les grignote"* (I am nibbling them). The strategy was obvious: the army that ran out of men first would be the loser. The wasteful local offensives would continue.

British troops seeking shelter in a mine crater, near Aubers Ridge, Artois, a section of the Labyrinth.

Imperial War Museum

Joffre had his autumn offensive planned, and Kitchener was with him. In trade for troops that were shipped off to Gallipoli, Joffre could count on Kitchener's agreement for an impressive co-ordinated offensive in Champagne. "A successful break-through both in Champagne and in Artois," he informed Sir John, "was to be followed immediately by a general offensive of all the French and British armies on the Western Front which will compel the Germans to retreat beyond the Meuse and possibly end the war." Joffre was ready to bite off another nibble.

New, young, fresh faces were drawn from the supply of reserves, though rapidly dwindling, and were brought to the Western Front to fill the spaces left by the thousands who had been killed or maimed. In Champagne, where Pétain was given a fifteen-mile front, preparations were made during the summer right under the observant eyes of the Germans. When nearly 2,000 guns of various sizes opened up along Pétain's front, the French intent was obvious. The Germans moved back and waited.

Street scene: Loos. The cost to the British Army—60,000 men.

National Archives

HMS Mauretania *in dazzle paint. The design supposedly confused submariners aiming torpedoes.*

Three days of roaring cannon later, on September 25, the French troops, assured by Joffre that their élan would be *"irrésistible,"* charged through a torrential rain. Despite the mud the French troops overran the abandoned first-line German trenches but gained little beyond that. Additional élan consisted of suicidal attacks on entrenched German positions, until in October Pétain called off the slaughter despite the wishes of his superiors. Even so, an attempt was made to breach the German second positions, with even worse results. The Champagne offensive was reduced to a whimper by November 8; for very little ground Joffre had traded about 150,000 Frenchmen (the German losses amounted to about 100,000).

On the same day that the ill-fated Champagne battle opened, September 25, the combined British and French assault began in Artois. Haig's troops hoped to take Loos and General Victor Louis d'Urbal's Tenth Army, jumping off from Souchez, hoped to gain in the autumn offensive the goal that had not been reached in the spring: Vimy Ridge. They nearly made it, but by the third day the terrain—they called it "The Labyrinth"—the weather, and the Germans cut them to pieces. True, German prisoners were taken, as they had been at Champagne, but at a horrendous cost: 190,000 Frenchmen for 120,000 Germans (about 18,000 of these were prisoners). The French back home heard only of the large roundup of German prisoners, not the grossly larger French casualties.

97

As for Loos, the British took it (although Haig, when he inspected the ground before the battle, predicted that it could not be done). He was overruled by Sir John French, who had to keep up good relations with Joffre, who protected him from Kitchener. Although there were initial British gains, French, who did not (with reason) trust Haig, denied the use of reserves until too late and the battle fizzled out. The B.E.F. lost 60,000 of their best at Loos.

German counterattacks, hindered by bad weather, only contributed to their casualty lists. But the Western Front, with insignificant indentations, hardly changed during 1915.

Haig, suspicious that Sir John French would lay the failure of Loos at his door, worked diligently behind his commander's back. He wrote letters; he had friends in high places (he came from the influential whisky family) and by December 15, Sir John French was back in London; he was replaced by Sir Douglas, now the British Commander-in-Chief of the B.E.F. in France. What was left of it.

For Britain the war at sea began as the war on land ended: badly. On New Year's Day the German submarine U-24 sank the battleship *Formidable* in home waters—always humiliating. But later in the month, January 24–25, the Royal Navy had its (limited) revenge. Rear Admi-

Big guns of the British Royal Navy. The Germans hoped to avoid them as much as possible.

Admiral David Beatty.

ral Franz von Hipper led a squadron of battle cruisers, light cruisers, and destroyers (twenty-seven in all) out of the German base at Wilhelmshaven and headed for British waters. The British were aware of this because of the lucky find by the Russians of the German codes and maps of the North Sea found in a sunken cruiser in the Baltic early in the war. Radio interception did the rest.

Under Admiral Beatty, the British arranged an interception of Hipper's ships at Dogger Bank in the North Sea about sixty miles off the English coast. With his force of forty-two ships, Beatty heavily outweighed the guns of the German ships.

When he sighted the approaching British, after an exchange of gunfire, Hipper realized that he was outgunned and ordered a fast return to Wilhelmshaven. Beatty's faster cruisers and destroyers began the pur-

Six-inch gun on the forward deck of the British Severn, *searching for the elusive cruiser* Königsberg (*which was eventually tracked to a port in German East Africa and sunk by ship gunfire and aircraft*).

The German cruiser Dresden, *caught by British ships in the Pacific off the coast of Chile, is sent to the bottom. The* Dresden *had eluded the Royal Navy at the Falkland Islands in December 1914.*

Engine room of a German submarine.

suit; after four hours the British began firing on the last ship in the German column, the battle cruiser *Blücher*. Beatty's flagship, *Lion*, turned its attention to *Seydlitz*, which took several hits and was heavily damaged and managed to flee.

The *Lion* too was hit and badly damaged, but continued the fight. *Blücher*, the most punished of the German ships, was eventually sunk, after Beatty was forced to leave the *Lion* out of the battle because of damages. A misunderstood order centered all the attention on the stricken *Blücher* as the rest of the German squadron slipped away. What might have been a more decisive British victory was costly to the Germans. The *Blücher* was lost, two other ships were damaged, and more than 950 seamen died. Two British ships suffered damages and fifteen sailors lost their lives. The fact that the British appeared to be waiting for the German squadron led to a general timidity in the High Seas Fleet and a greater dependence on the submarine.

German U-boat submerging, photographed by a patrolling airship.

A British submarine under attack by German aircraft.

The prelude to unleashing the U-boats was Germany's announcement that after February 18 the waters around Britain were a war zone, meaning that even merchant ships would be attacked there without warning. In March, Britain announced a blockade of Germany; this would result, eventually, in near starvation for German civilians.

The U-boat war took a dramatic turn on May 7. The Cunard liner *Lusitania,* which had sailed from New York carrying 1,918 passengers, some cargo (including ammunition), but unarmed, was attacked without warning by U-20 in the Irish Sea. Commander Walther Schweiger placed two torpedoes into the ship's hull and eighteen minutes later the great liner rested on the bottom. More than a thousand lives (including more than 400 women and children) were lost; only 640 passengers were saved. More than a hundred Americans perished, including such celebrities as millionaire Alfred Gwynne Vanderbilt, Broadway pro-

A British merchant ship at the moment that a torpedo from the U-boat (in foreground) has hit a vital spot.

103

568

*As a torpedoed ship noses down, some members of the crew
in a lifeboat attempt to pull away. Dangling ropes enabled
the men to slide into the water.*

ducer Charles Frohman, and popular essayist ("A Message to Garcia")
Elbert Hubbard. But even more significant so far as the impact on the
world was concerned was the phrase "women and children," who were
killed in frightful numbers by the U-20.

The effect upon an America hoping to remain neutral was one of rag-
ing shock. Public opinion shifted in favor of the Allies. President
Woodrow Wilson, though he sent strongly worded communications to
the German Government, refused to be stampeded. He loftily made the
statement, "There is such a thing as a man being too proud to fight,"
and continued to steer the United States along a neutral course.

The outcry had some effect in Germany too, where it was suggested
that the U-boat campaign be curtailed, but Admiral Tirpitz stood fast.
Warnings had appeared in newspapers before the *Lusitania* had sailed
and the ship had gone down in those waters the Germans had decreed
were a war zone; a special commemorative medal was even cast cele-

104

brating the U-20's feat. The British reproduced it as an indication of German callousness; in the United States, the cry of "Remember the *Lusitania!*" was heard. But after a brief interval, while the Kaiser pondered the U-boat problem and submarine activity lessened, Tirpitz prevailed.

In August the White Star liner *Arabic* was torpedoed without warning and sunk on its way from Liverpool to New York (thirty-two missing, two of them Americans); in November an Austrian submarine sank the Italian liner *Ancona,* bound for New York from Naples (312 missing, some of whom may have been American). Wilson dispatched a blistering note demanding an explanation and the punishment of the submarine's captain; he was successful in this, but the U-boat war went on.

The Germans continued to suffer a bad press during the closing months of 1915. In October the world was shocked by the news that a British nurse, Edith Cavell, serving in occupied Brussels, had been executed by a firing squad for helping Allied wounded escape. The news of this stimulated enlistments in Britain—the number announced was

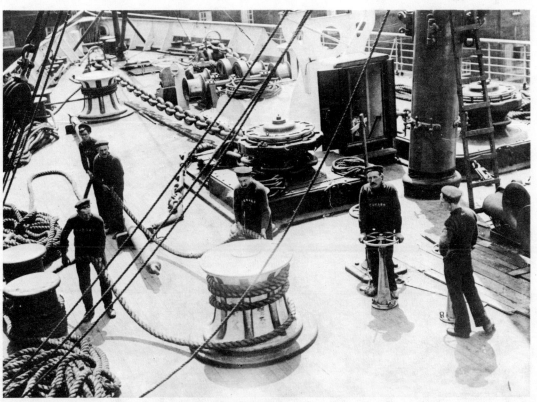

National Archives

Deckhands of the SS Lusitania, *the Cunard Line's luxury ocean liner—the "Fastest and Largest Steamer in Atlantic Service"—whose passengers boarded the ship knowing of the German warning in the morning's papers.*

10,000. On the same front page of the New York *Times* dated October 25, 1915, the arrest of two Germans was reported; one of them, Robert Fay, was an officer in the German Army, a veteran of the Marne, and associated with the German Foreign Ministry. Fay and one Robert Scholz were caught with a supply of explosives which they planned, it was reported, to plant aboard ships leaving New York Harbor.

Such revelations—the sequel to the Belgian atrocities—and the submarine warfare did not improve relations between Germany and the United States.

---- ·⊰()⊱· ----

An even more exotic, and thus romantic—and romanticized—arena of war became more evident in 1915: the air. When the war began, aircraft were regarded with disdain and suspicion by professional soldiers. To the dismay of cavalrymen the first military planes were used to observe enemy movements, usually the cavalry's job. The planes were not armed and frequently enemy airmen exchanged friendly greetings as they passed one another in the sky on their respective missions.

National Archives

Tugboats gather round the sleek 31,000-ton Lusitania *in New York's harbor. It is now known that the* Lusitania *did, in fact, carry a cargo of war matériel; its detonation caused the* Lusitania *to sink within twenty minutes.*

Les Atrocités Allemandes

— Un lieutenant-colonel du corps expéditionnaire en France, écrit à la date du 29 Avril 1915 : — Les Allemands ont crucifié un soldat canadien qu'ils avaient fait prisonnier.

(RAPPORT OFFICIEL ANGLAIS).

German atrocities in Belgium, 1915: this drawing dramatizes the "official report" of a British officer describing the crucifixion of a Canadian prisoner of war.

An "official Belgian report" describes German torture of a Belgian youth.

Les Atrocités Allemandes

— A Wacherzel, un jeune garçon est déshabillé jusqu'à la taille, attaché à un arbre, et on s'amuse à le piquer du bout des sabres, à faire de son torse mince une cible...

(RAPPORT OFFICIEL BELGE).

"KEEP THE HOME FIRES BURNING" — 1915

One day it dawned on someone that the information the enemy carried could be used in planning battles. Airmen began carrying rifles and pistols to take potshots at one another, generally with little result, but it did end the camaraderie of the air. In time even bricks and other destructive materials were carried to deal with enemy aircraft. Eventually machine guns were mounted on the planes, and when formations of these "scouts" met over the trenches, the men below were treated to the drama of a "dogfight"—even the thrilling sight of a plane falling in flames.

By 1915 the flying machine had evolved into a fighting machine and with it a curious star system. Germans in their Fokkers, Frenchmen in their Nieuports, and British in their B.E.2s (called "Quirks," no doubt because they had so many) began making names for themselves and, if lucky or very skilled, began chalking up victories. Eventually a fighter pilot who shot down five enemy aircraft became, though not officially, an "ace," a system of recognition first used by the French. The leading

National Archives

*This chalice, retaken from a German trench, was supposedly stolen
from a French cathedral and used as a beer stein,
and the cover used as an ashtray.*

108

German air fighters of 1915. Postcards such as this were sold widely in Germany during the war; aviators were especially popular. Two of Germany's early aerial stars: Oswald Boelcke (front row, fourth from left) and Max Immelmann (front row, third from right). Neither survived the war.

French pilots with a mechanic stand in front of their plane; early two-seaters were generally used for reconnassance flights and were not armed.

Georges Guynemer (center) and mechanic. Guynemer became the most celebrated of all French aces. Though ill, he managed through family influence to get into the air service. Almost suicidal in air fighting, he quickly ran up a large total of victories over German airmen.

German air celebrity of the early phase of the air war was Oswald Boelcke, whose "score," before he perished in an air accident, had reached forty. An early French airman who had a large following was the sickly Georges Guynemer, who destroyed more than fifty German planes before he, then the French *as des as* (ace of aces), perished in 1917.

The best known British pilots of 1915 were those who took on the fearful menace, the Zeppelin. These great dirigibles, ranging in length from 400 to 700 feet, penetrated the night sky over England dropping bombs on a terrified populace. This was Germany's revenge for the British blockade and was intended to spread terror in Britain. The fact is, the Zeppelin raids accomplished very little militarily and did not particularly panic the English.

It would take the advocates of the airship as a weapon some time to realize that they were slow and could be readily overtaken by the speedier fighter planes—and tracked by antiaircraft guns; their bulk placed them at the mercy of the winds, making navigation and the precise placement of bombs questionable. But both the German Navy and Army dispatched these "Monsters of the Purple Twilight" to England to

110

sow fright. German school children were taught the words to a song that defined the mission of the airships:

Zeppelin, flieg,
Hilf uns im Krieg,
Fliege nach England,
England wird abgebrannt,
Zeppelin, flieg.

(Fly, Zeppelin,
Help us win the war,
Fly against England,
England will be consumed by fire,
Fly, Zeppelin.)

The airship raids against England began the night of January 19, 1915, when three raiders appeared over East Anglia; twenty civilians were killed or injured. When the year's attacks ended on the night of October 13, the "accomplishments" were not impressive. Out of a total of twenty-two raids (in which fifty-five airships participated) some damage was done, 208 died, and 532 were injured. Although London was regarded as a legitimate military target, many missions failed to reach the capital and the bombs fell haphazardly, snuffing out the lives of small numbers of civilians (the first airship to reach London did not arrive until August).

During the 1915 airship raids the Germans paid heavily for such warmaking. The Navy's L-8 was forced down by gunfire over Belgium and was lost. In June, Sub-Lieutenant R. A. J. Warneford, aloft in a tiny but bomb-laden Morane monoplane, spotted the LZ-37, homeward bound after bombing Hull. Warneford had taken off hoping to attack Zeppelin sheds across the lines from Belgium. Instead, he bombed the slow-moving LZ-37, which detonated and fell burning to the ground near Ghent; only one member of the crew survived the flaming fall. Other airships were lost that year; one was struck by lightning; another, the L-12, had been hit by gunfire over Britain and burned while being dismantled at Ostend (the airships burned easily because they were inflated with hydrogen).

When the 1915 campaign ended, although the Zeppelin Menace had managed to reach London, nothing had been gained militarily. The Germans had merely produced another weapon that made headlines around the world and diminished their stature internationally; the word "Hun" was in common usage. Airship crews were called "baby killers"; while military targets were their objectives, precision bombing was not even

111

remotely possible, considering the state of navigational and bomb-sighting equipment at the time.

Bombs frequently fell into empty fields, into crowded cities, so that civilians, noncombatants, were the victims, not professional soldiers. Dwellings, not munitions factories, were demolished. Airship commanders dropped bombs, mistaking one place for another, or out of fear and the hope to jettison and return to base. On one raid the L-15, commanded by one of the celebrities among the Zeppelin commanders, Heinrich Mathy, never reached its objective, London. Mathy planted the bombload instead on Guildford and did manage to make a small break in the London and South Western Railway—and killed one enemy swan.

By the end of 1915 the Great War's greatness was highly tarnished. The "civilized world" had become a Giant Slaughterhouse.

Zeppelins L-10, L-12, and L-13 setting out on a raid, August 9, 1915 (the photo was taken from the L-11). Over Britain the L-12 was hit by gunfire, returned to Ostend for repairs, and burned during dismantling.

Douglas H. Robinson Collection

Germans on the Russian-Polish Front going to the aid of their troubled ally, Austria.

A Russian fortification at Przemysl which was taken from the Austrians in 1914 and reoccupied by the Germans in June 1915.

Spoils of war: Germans sifting through captured matériel for future use.

A new battleground: with the entry of Italy into the war on the Allied side, yet another battlefield came into focus. An Austrian rifleman on the frontier peers down into Italy near Mori.

General Maurice Sarrail, commander of "The Army of the Orient," and keeper of the "Bird Cage" at Salonika. Arrogant, undiplomatic, Sarrail accomplished practically nothing militarily at Salonika from October 1915 until December 1917, when he was relieved.

Falkenhayn, the new German Commander-in-Chief, though a confirmed Western Fronter, moved to the east to keep an eye on Hindenburg and Ludendorff, his rivals for command.

First Lord of the Admiralty, Winston Churchill, who did not agree with First Sea Lord John Fisher on the wisdom of attempting to take the Dardanelles by sea power alone.

French reinforcements for Gallipoli, Moudros Harbor, Lemnos Island in the Aegean; they would participate in the landings on Cape Helles in April—to little avail.

Australians at Anzac beachhead in a fruitless attempt to rush the Turkish positions at Sari-Bair.

*As a shell from "Asiatic Annie" explodes near the beach of
Cape Helles, British troops casually seek the shelter of
the cliffs that lined the road.*

British troops evacuating Suvla Bay, Gallipoli, December 1915.

King George V on an inspection tour; the troops are South African and will serve in a labor corps.

Germans constructing a bombproof shelter in Flanders. With the coming of rain this earth turned to knee-deep mud.

French poilus *on guard in the quiet Alsace sector. Their small hut is supposedly camouflaged from enemy airmen, but appears to be rather thumblike in this terrain.*

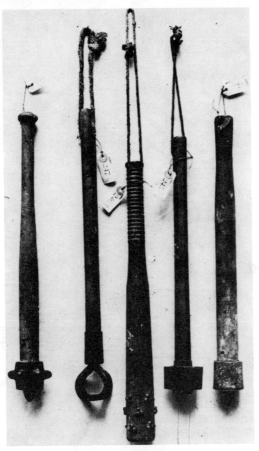

*Back to the caveman:
clubs used in close
combat in trench raids.*

*Back to the Middle Ages:
protective armor used by Allied
soldiers in the early phase
of the war. It was of
little help if a soldier
wished to move quickly.*

*An early form of gas mask issued to British soldiers in
May 1915, after the Germans used poison gas on the Western
Front for the first time at Ypres, April 22, 1915.*

ADVERTISEMENT.

NOTICE!

TRAVELLERS intending to embark on the Atlantic voyage are reminded that a state of war exists between Germany and her allies and Great Britain and her allies; that the zone of war includes the waters adjacent to the British Isles; that, in accordance with formal notice given by the Imperial German Government, vessels flying the flag of Great Britain, or of any of her allies, are liable to destruction in those waters and that travellers sailing in the war zone on ships of Great Britain or her allies do so at their own risk.

IMPERIAL GERMAN EMBASSY
WASHINGTON, D. C., APRIL 22, 1915.

A notice placed by the German Embassy in several American newspapers. In New York it appeared just below an announcement by Cunard that their Lusitania was leaving for Liverpool on Saturday May 1.

Admiral Alfred von Tirpitz, architect of the German High Seas Fleet and advocate of unrestricted submarine warfare. He commanded the German Navy at the beginning of the war and resigned in March 1916 because a tough submarine campaign was not being waged to his liking.

Depth charge, one method of dealing with the submarine menace. Properly placed, the charge could crush the hull of a submarine.

Poster inspired by the sinking of the Lusitania.

The well-dressed airman, 1915. An American volunteer, Kiffin Rockwell, serving with the Paris Air Guard, models cold weather clothing.

*Sub-Lieutenant R. A. J. Warneford, who discovered a method for dealing
with the Zeppelin menace: he flew over the airship
and dropped a bomb on it.*

The Morane monoplane from which Warneford destroyed the LZ-37.

*Assorted sizes of bombs carried
by marauding Zeppelins.*

Western Front, 1915: British dug into a blasted landscape, near Vimy Ridge.

1916
"There's a Long, Long Trail"

EARLY in December 1915, Joffre called for an international conference at his headquarters in Chantilly, during which he proposed coordinated all-out offensives by the Allies—Britain, Russia, Italy, and France. Just before the year ended he summoned Haig and proposed a plan for a combined offensive on a sixty-mile front on the Somme. Haig was not happy, for as he saw it, a great battle on the Somme would achieve little if anything. He had his eye on Flanders and the hope to push the Germans out of Belgium. Joffre diplomatically did not insist but went about making his plans.

These were spoiled by Falkenhayn, who had returned to his favorite front, leaving the Eastern Front in the hands of his rivals, Hindenburg and Ludendorff. Although Falkenhayn regarded the British as the "archenemy," he felt that with his forces tied up in the east, he did not have the manpower to challenge the British head-on. Instead, he chose to finish off Britain's primary ally, France. After the wholesale killing of 1915, he sensed that the French were growing sick of war. His plan was to attack some point on the French line that might be chipped away gradually by the Germans, but that the French would be compelled to defend patriotically and literally to the last man. Falkenhayn planned to keep the German sacrifice minimal while France bled to death; he would employ the greatest artillery barrages the world had ever known; he would make no attempt to make any great advances. But a steady pressure would be applied to the French troops on the modest front he had selected. The French would send in their soldiers to be ground up by German guns. Falkenhayn studied the map for a likely place: should it be Belfort or Verdun?

Falkenhayn's decision and Joffre's plan for the Somme would make 1916 a year of monstrous, monotonous death.

125

French Embassy Press & Information Division

The result of German artillery bombardment of the town of Verdun, through which supplies to the forts that circled it were transported.

Falkenhayn struck first; he chose to batter the wedge in the front at Verdun. Early in the morning of February 21 about a thousand big German guns began pulverizing the French positions along an eight-mile front. Six German divisions were poised to rush into the French strongholds as soon as the barrage lifted in the afternoon. One German aviator flying over the region during the bombardment was shocked by the fury of the attack. The French earth looked like a photograph of the moon. "There won't be anything living out there," the aviator observed. He was wrong.

What the Germans did not know was that Joffre had defused the more than dozen obsolescent forts around Verdun, certain that the main fighting would occur farther north. Most of the forts were stripped of their guns and manned by reduced crews (only two French divisions faced the Germans at Verdun).

When the barrage lifted short of Verdun and the German infantry moved into the first positions with their rifles slung over their shoulders, they were certain that nothing lived in the devastated area. But there

126

1916

GREAT BRITAIN

IRELAND
Dublin

London

NORTH SEA

BEATTY
Rosyth
E FLOW
SCHEER
× BATTLE OF JUTLAND
SKAGERRAK

DENMARK

SWEDEN

BALTIC SEA

NETHERLANDS

ENGLISH CHANNEL

BELGIUM
LUX.
Ypres
Arras
SOMME

Hamburg

Berlin

GERMANY

RHINE

STALEMATED FRONT

Paris
Verdun
MARNE
SEINE
LOIRE

FRANCE

Bordeaux
GARONNE

BAY OF BISCAY

SPAIN

Lyon
RHONE

Marseille

SWITZERLAND
Trentino
Rovereto
ELEVENTH
Po

ITALY
Rome

SARDINIA

Vienna
DANUBE

AUSTRIA-HUNGARY

Gorizia

Warsaw

Kaunas

Vilna

Riga

R   U   S   S   I   A

PRIPET MARSHES

Pinsk

THIRD
EIGHTH
ELEVENTH
SEVENTH
Czernowitz
NINTH

BRUSILOV

Lemberg

DNIESTER
PRUT
BUG

Kiev
DNIEPER

Moscow

OKA
VOLGA
DON
Rostov

VOLGA

CASPIAN SEA

Tiflis

BLACK SEA

RUMANIA
FALKENHAYN
Ploesti
Bucharest
DANUBE
MACKENSEN
Sofia
BULGARIA
SERBIA
Belgrade
Monastir
MONTENEGRO
ALBANIA
SAVA

ADRIATIC SEA

Odessa
Constanta

Constantinople
DARDANELLES
GALLIPOLI PENINSULA
Angora
Smyrna
BRITISH EVACUATION
JAN.

SALONIKA (FR.)
(SERB.) (BR.)
GREECE
Athens

CRETE

MEDITERRANEAN SEA

MALTA
SICILY

TUNISIA
Tunis
Algiers
ALGERIA

LIBYA

YUDENICH (RUS.)
Erzerum
Trebizond
Bayburt
THIRD (TURK.)
Erzincan

T   U   R   K   E   Y

TIGRIS
EUPHRATES

CYPRUS

SYRIA
PALESTINE
Jerusalem
KRESSENSTEIN (TURK.)
El Arish
Romani
MURRAY
EGYPT
SUEZ CANAL

Tabriz
PERSIA
Tokerau
Hamadan
BARATOV (RUS.)
Khanikin

MESOPOTAMIA
Baghdad
Kut-el-Amara
TOWNSHEND SURRENDERS
MAUDE
Nasiriya
Basra

PERSIAN GULF

ARABIA
HUSSEIN REVOLTS, MECCA AND MEDINA TAKEN

MILES 400
KM 400
N
E
S
W

palacios

were survivors who stumbled out of their bunkers and trenches. Some were in shock, but others were capable of firing rifles, machine guns, and the accurate, fast-firing French 75s. On some portions of the front the Germans were mowed down by the survivors—until they themselves were killed. Falkenhayn was right, the French intended to hold Verdun.

The *poilus* held on stubbornly, some dying in their bunkers, burned alive by the new weapon the Germans had developed, the flamethrower. The Germans, inching toward Verdun, died too. On February 25 they took Fort Douaumont, the major link in the Verdun system, with very little effort. There were fewer than sixty men holding the degunned fort (in its heyday Douaumont would have been defended by more than 500 men). On the eastern flank of the front, some French units withdrew to the Heights of the Meuse.

Joffre immediately threatened any commander who retreated with a court-martial. He also sent for Pétain to take command of the battle. Calmly Pétain went about compensating for Joffre's Verdun mistakes.

At Verdun, a French dugout, providing shelter from German aircraft active over the area.

Crown Prince Wilhelm, son of the Kaiser, who was selected by
Falkenhayn to carry out his plan to draw French blood into the
Verdun area. The Crown Prince commanded the German Fifth Army.
With him: one of his divisional commanders, General Max von Gallwitz.

He organized the defenses, demanded reinforcements and equipment, and brought order to what was a chaotic situation.

To supply his front, Pétain depended primarily on a single road that ran from Bar-le-Duc, forty miles south of Verdun. (The railroads running into the fortress were insufficient and often under attack by German artillery.) To bring in men and supplies, Pétain transformed the old secondary road into a belt line of trucks, some 3,000 of them moving continuously into and out of Verdun day and night. This lone artery of supply over which nearly 200,000 Frenchmen were transported into the charterhouse of Verdun was named by them La Voie Sacrée (The Sacred Way).

The Germans had a much superior communications system behind their lines, several railroads over which fresh German troops and supplies were siphoned into the narrow Verdun front. At either end,

129

*Street scene, Ypres. The British stubbornly continued to
hold the salient even as Haig prepared for
his big push on the Somme.*

French or German, the youth of the nation were jammed into what
Pétain called "the Furnace of Verdun" and were consumed.

Joffre, realizing he was in trouble, called for help from the Allies. The
British responded by taking over a portion of the front near Arras, freeing yet another French division for the Furnace; Italy complied with yet
another of the fruitless series of attacks against the Austrians on the
Isonzo front and the Russians sacrificed over 100,000 green troops in
the battle of Lake Naroch late in March.

After a brief lull the battle at Verdun flared up again when Crown
Prince Wilhelm, commanding the German Fifth Army, shifted his main
effort to the left flank of the salient on the west bank of the Meuse. The
Germans pushed toward Hill 304 and another hill, appropriately named
Le Mort Homme, about nine miles northwest of Verdun. Both were
under German control by the end of May, but to what strategic end no
one could say. On the right flank the Crown Prince's troops took Fort
Vaux, closing another epic of French resistance on June 7. So impressed
was the Crown Prince with the stand that he ceremoniously presented

130

the commander, Major Sylvain-Eugène Raynal, with a pair of infantry wire cutters (until a real sword could be found). To permit a vanquished enemy to keep his sword was regarded as a high honor among military men.

The occupation of Forts Vaux and Douaumont did not end the slaughter at Verdun. On June 20 the Germans tried again, employing a new form of gas shell, containing diphosgene, and managed to push up to Belleville heights, but Verdun itself held. Falkenhayn had failed except in his desire to bleed France.

But there had been some changes on the French side; some shifts in command brought two aggressive generals to the scene. Pétain was put in command of the Central Army Group and General Robert Nivelle took over the Second Army; they were joined by a tough infantryman, General Charles Mangin. Attempts to go over to the offensive did not regain the lost forts, but events on other fronts did bring relief—the Italians were on the counteroffensive at Trentino; the Russians, under Aleksei Brusilov, had launched a massive offensive in the east; and in July the great attack that Joffre had planned earlier in the year erupted on the Somme.

Falkenhayn was forced to call a halt to the German nibblings at Verdun and withdraw troops for the Eastern Front. He was further distracted by the great British effort on the Somme.

But the battle of attrition continued as each side chopped away at the other. Finally, with French reinforcements, Mangin directed a counterattack, which opened on October 24, and took back Fort Douaumont; by November the Germans abandoned Fort Vaux. On December 15, Mangin and Nivelle attacked on a six-mile front and within three days had taken over 10,000 German prisoners and pushed the Germans back two miles, virtually to the line at which the epic, but pointless, battle had begun in February.

Though nothing had been gained in the roughly ten months of fighting, there were certain indelible consequences: between them Germany and France lost 700,000 men, each contributing about half (though France's losses were a bit higher) to the shocking casualty lists.

There were further consequences of Verdun. In August, when it became obvious that Falkenhayn had failed, Hindenburg and Ludendorff were ordered from the east to take command on the Western Front. Even the fat head of Joffre rolled; in December he was relieved as Commander-in-Chief and the man everyone believed had saved Verdun, Nivelle, replaced him.

But the blood flow on the Western Front was not ended when Falkenhayn was recalled. Joffre's Grand Offensive, fruit of the Chantilly conference in December 1915, finally ripened on July 1, 1916, on the Somme. It was Britain's turn to bleed.

131

King George V arrives to observe a battle from a hill near Fricourt.
From that point he saw two Australian divisions take
Pozières on the Albert-Bapaume Road, Somme, 1916.

Although some historians claim that the battle on the Somme saved Verdun, others say that Verdun was responsible for what happened on the Somme. It is true that the Allied offensive in July distracted Falkenhayn's attention from his bloodbath at Verdun, but with France's military might being poured into Verdun, the July offensive became primarily a British operation.

General Sir Henry Rawlinson's Fourth Army was positioned on the left bank of the Somme on a front of about fifteen miles; the French Sixth Army, on the right bank, covered a narrower front. There were fourteen British and five French divisions facing six German divisions. The preponderance went for nothing, for the Germans had spent the quiet months in their sector digging into the chalky soil of Picardy, planting barbed wire, and constructing a complex and efficient trench system.

Word of the impending Big Push had begun to circulate in the spring, but no surprise was really intended. Before the battle began the entire front was battered by more than 1,500 Allied guns and a million and a half artillery shells of assorted calibers. This continued for a week. In the morning of July 1 the Allied troops went over the top. The French made some headway, but for Haig's British troops, which included the last of the regulars that had survived Ypres and Loos as well as fresh

132

conscripts (for the first time in its history, Britain began drafting its soldiers in January 1916). It was the death of an army.

July 1 was described by a participant in the battle as "a day of intense blue summer beauty, full of roaring violence, and a confusion of death, agony, and triumph, from dawn till dark." And it was the day on which the outcome of the battle was determined. Of the 110,000 British troops who went over the top, 60,000 were casualties (about a third of whom were dead or dying in No Man's Land) by dark. If Haig could note in his diary, "Our troops had everywhere crossed the enemy's front trenches," it was too early for him to realize that barbed wire, machine guns, and German artillery cut them down in those trenches. Most of these members of "Kitchener's Army" would never return.

The amateur soldiers, most of them from the working classes of the Midlands, were sent into No Man's Land burdened down with sixty-six pounds of equipment and marched in neatly assembled "waves" into machine-gun fire from the quickly recovered German positions. Since the Germans held higher ground, the advancing British were under constant surveillance by German spotters.

And so the battle that had been decided on the first day, like Verdun, ground on. Rawlinson attempted a nighttime attack on July 14 but was unable to exploit the advantages of the surprise with his cavalry as planned. The skirmishing only added to the toll, German and English.

Aleksei Brusilov, the Russian general who, for a time, caused concern in the Austrian-German command and also depleted the Czar's army.

Imperial War Museum

Haig, desperate to cut down on his wholesale losses to the murderous machine guns, gambled on Britain's new secret weapon. He ignored the arguments that the weapon was not yet completely tested or its operators fully trained. He even ignored the fact that there were too few available —forty-nine in all—to prove decisive.

So it was that on September 15, the weapon code-named the "tank," was introduced on the Western Front. Eighteen tanks were shipped to the front and, after breakdowns, about ten clanked toward the fearful Germans. While these strange monsters could withstand machine-gun fire, crushed barbed-wire entanglements, and had a psychological effect on the Germans (one tank crew took more than 300 prisoners), there were too few to decide the battle. And the secret was out. The Germans admitted that the tank was, indeed, one of the most effective weapons of the war, but knowing they existed enabled them to contend with them. One method that worked frightfully was the flamethrower.

The Somme battle ground away with attack, counterattack, and little gained; with the coming of the winter rains the pulverized earth turned to lakes of mud in which neither man nor beast could function. The British, obstinately, made a final push in November, but by the eighteenth the battle on the Somme was ended.

The Allies had gained about 125 square miles of ground of no strategic value; they had advanced on a thirty-mile front, with the deepest penetration no more than seven miles. The cost: 420,000 British casualties, 204,000 French, and 670,000 German. It had not been merely the winter rains that ended the battle; the antagonists were, as Ludendorff would later recall in his memoirs, "utterly exhausted."

The major battles on the Eastern Front in 1916 were designed as diversionary support to the Allies, which ultimately harmed the Russians more than it helped the Allies. The year's surprise Russian victory, in fact, turned into a disaster.

The French appealed to Czar Nicholas to harry the Germans and relieve some of the pressure at Verdun. Obligingly the self-proclaimed Russian Commander-in-Chief launched an offensive on March 19 in the vicinity of Lake Naroch, near the northern end of the front. The Russians attacked on the German-held front of about ninety miles, following an artillery barrage. The Germans had not wasted their time on the quiet front; well dug in, they machine-gunned the Russian troops sloshing through the freezing water that covered the iced-over lake; those who escaped the machine guns were chopped up by artillery or gassed. The battle at Lake Naroch gained nothing for Verdun and lost the Czar 100,000 soldiers (the German loss: about 20,000).

Those Russian troops lost in March were therefore unavailable when the time came to co-ordinate a Russian offensive with Joffre's Big Push (actually Haig's) on the Somme. But before Haig got moving, the Czar

Imperial War Museum

Commander of the Danube Army, Mackensen, who upset Rumanian war plans. He rides into Bucharest after troops comanded by the former Chief of Staff, Falkenhayn, took the city in November 1916.

heeded yet another call for help, this time from a harried Italy. Conrad's Austro-Hungarian armies had begun moving on the Trentino flank, and the Italians hoped that Russian pressure could draw away some of Conrad's forces.

By this time the Russians had 130 divisions on their front facing 86 German and Austrian divisions; numbers did not count much, for although the Russians could assemble the manpower, they were sadly lacking in firepower. In compliance with the Italian request, the Czar assigned the task of assaulting the German-Austrian line to his able General Aleksei Brusilov, who commanded the Russian armies south of the Pripet Marshes to the Rumanian border.

On June 4, Brusilov struck along a 200-mile Austrian-held part of the front; the Austrian Fourth and Seventh armies, surprised and overwhelmed, collapsed. Within the first three days the Russians rounded up 200,000 prisoners. The "Brusilov Offensive," as it came to be called (the only operation of the war named for its commander), appeared to promise victory—for a while.

Though launched prematurely to coincide with the fighting at the Somme, Brusilov's Offensive did do something for the Allies. A frightened Conrad withdrew Austrian divisions from the Trentino, which brought an end to that drive, and Falkenhayn withdrew several German divisions from Verdun. These German troops, plus the denial to Brusi-

135

lov of reserves from the armies on the northern part of the line and the terrible Russian supply problem, determined the final outcome of the offensive.

By the end of June it had begun to run out of steam because of the heavy loss of men and equipment, but after lulls it flared again in August and September, reaching its fullest penetration of the Austrian-German lines, where it finally exhausted itself. Brusilov was hailed as a great hero, and then reality set in: in exchange for 600,000 Germans and Austrians, the Russians lost a million troops, including reserves. Brusilov's Offensive had succeeded in destroying an army—his own. Depleted, almost extinct, it was by October 1916 ripe for revolt.

One other drastic effect of the brief, false victory of the Brusilov Offensive was the entry, on the Allied side, of Rumania as a belligerent. Linked by treaty with Austria when the war began, the Rumanians bided their time before leaping. Pressured from both sides, Rumanian politicians and diplomats adroitly remained neutral for two years. But the mirage of an Allied victory and of territorial gains (Transylvania) in Austria-Hungary and Bulgaria, tipped the scales. The Allies hoped that the Rumanians would concentrate their half-million-man army on Bulgaria and move southward to free Sarrail's troops cooped up in the Bird Cage of Salonika.

But Rumanian eyes were on the riches of Transylvania, and on August 27, General Alexandru Averescu struck. Once again the Austrian Army fell back, but only for a while. The Central Powers were, in fact, ready for the Rumanian move. Under General August von Mackensen the Danube Army (Bulgarians, Turks, and Germans) was formed while the Rumanian forces moved cautiously into Transylvania. The Austrians retreated, blowing up bridges behind them, as five German and two Austrian divisions were rushed in. They were established on the Maros River, ready for the counterattack.

Falkenhayn, only recently relieved as Commander-in-Chief on the Western Front, was in full command of the Rumanian operation. He struck on September 5, when Mackensen's Danube Army moved in from Bulgaria in the south. The Danube Army destroyed three poorly trained and badly equipped Rumanian divisions and then turned eastward, heading for the Dobruja region on the Black Sea. This served to disrupt the Rumanian plans for Transylvania, diverting reserves intended for that front to the south.

Falkenhayn then lashed out at the faltering Rumanians in Transylvania on September 27. His Ninth Army consisted of five divisions (three of them German) and the Austrian First Army mustered another five (one German); by the twenty-ninth they had retaken Hermannstadt (now Sibiu), then on October 8 they drove the Rumanians out of Kronstadt (now Brasov). Meanwhile Mackensen continued to destroy the

Rumanians in the Dobruja, brushing aside the few Russian troops that had been sent to aid them. The approach of winter, which could especially hinder Falkenhayn in the mountain passes, contributed to the driving force of the Germans as they pushed for Bucharest.

On October 22, Mackensen took the important Black Sea port of Constanta. After winning the battle at Kronstadt, Falkenhayn, whose leadership in the Rumanian campaign may have caused the Kaiser to wish he had kept him as Commander-in-Chief, smashed his way through the Vulcan Pass onto the Walachian plain. Co-ordinating his movements with Falkenhayn's, Mackensen turned some of his units around and established a beachhead across the Danube; Bucharest lay less than thirty miles away. The remainder of the Danube Army continued to drive the Rumanians out of the Dobruja toward the Ukraine.

Falkenhayn unrelentingly turned aside a Rumanian counterattack in December; by the sixth his troops had taken Bucharest. The Government hastily fled to a new capital at Jassy. The Austro-German armies had almost completely overrun Rumania. Besides the capital they occupied rich farmlands and, for the purpose of making war, the rich Ploesti oil fields. Except for the northern province of Moldavia, Rumania was in the possession of the Central Powers.

The gamble for the riches of Transylvania had backfired. The Rumanian Army was shattered—more than 300,000 lost (only about half of these were taken prisoner); German losses totaled about 60,000, which, when added to those of the other fronts, was a drain on German manpower, victory or not.

During the ill-fated Rumanian campaign, the aged Emperor Franz Joseph of Austria died at eighty-six, one of the last of the Old World monarchs. He was succeeded by a great-nephew, Charles. The change in regime resulted in changes at the Austrian military top. Charles, who believed that there was too much German influence in Austria-Hungary, dismissed his Chief of Staff, Conrad, and replaced him with General Artur Arz von Straussenburg.

There was some activity in the Macedonian Bird Cage to the south at Salonika; Sarrail commanded a mixed army of British, French, Serbian, Italian, and Russian troops. The Serbs arrived in April and May, and although they initially impressed the British and French very little, they would prove to be savage fighters. Politically the situation was embarrassing to the Allies and the Greeks, although there was some co-operation from the Greek military if not the Government. It was a delicate situation that Sarrail did not handle delicately; he bulled ahead—though slowly—as if his troops were guests, not invaders. His occupation of Salonika had no effect on Verdun and little on the fortunes of Rumania.

But before Sarrail moved, the Bulgarians lashed out on August 17

137

Italian mountain troops in Trentino, where in May 1916 the
Austrians drove through the line—temporarily.

and soon a great Bulgarian victory was announced to the world. However, the Serbians under Sarrail soon recovered and struck back. Although aided by an Italian division and a Russian brigade, the Serbians proved the most dogged fighters in the rugged mountain country of the Greek-Bulgarian-Serbian frontier. The Bulgarians were driven back through the Monastir Gap, through which they had invaded Greece. The Germans quickly formed two divisions (with some troops drained off from the Western Front) and went to the aid of the Bulgars. But the Serbs, now back in their homeland, fought ferociously and prevailed despite the terrible weather and terrain. By November 19, Serbian and French troops entered Monastir (now Bitolj, Yugoslavia) inside Serbia. The advance, more than twenty-five miles, ended there with the virtual destruction of the Bulgarian First Army. Casualties were high, however; the Allies lost about 50,000 and the Bulgarians and Germans 60,000. Except for proving that the once defeated Serbian soldier was a tough and brave warrior, the battle accomplished little, a thrice-told tale so far as the battles of 1916 went. It was almost always a matter of much ventured and little gained.

On the secondary or colonial fronts the British fared poorly. The Gallipoli evacuation was completed in January; in April, Townshend finally surrendered Kut-el-Amara in Mesopotamia. This was followed by a lull during which the British forces were rebuilt, a new commander, Lieutenant General Sir Stanley Maude, came in, and once again British eyes focused on Baghdad. (Unlike the hapless Townshend, Maude would eventually reach that historic city.)

The end of Gallipoli released Turkish troops, a threat to the British in Egypt. Nervous over the possibility of Turkish occupation of the Suez Canal, the British commander, General Sir Archibald Murray (who had once served as the deposed Sir John French's Chief of Staff), prepared for such a contingency with elaborate fortifications of the canal, railway extensions, and a water pipeline, so necessary in the desert. Murray's error was that he overestimated the number of German-led Turks threatening the canal and the difficulty of large numbers of troops crossing the Sinai desert. He worried about the quarter million Turks (how he conjured up that generous number was a mystery) despite the difficulties he encountered with his own preparations even with superior technologies.

Murray's plan was to jump off from Suez, push east and then northward across the Sinai, invade Palestine, and assure safety of the canal. His preparations were interrupted by an attack led by the audacious German General Kress von Kressenstein (whose troops numbered 15,000) over a blistering desert in the appalling summer heat. His objective was the railhead at Romani. Though evenly matched in numbers, the British had logistics and short supply lines on their side. They stopped and turned back the Turkish-German troops by early August, although the bulk of the enemy forces slipped away into the desert.

Murray went back to business as usual, lumbering onward to Palestine, building his lines of communication and water supply as he moved. It was slow, hard work, but on December 21 the British took the Turkish outpost at El Arish; two days later Magdhaba was secured. The British now held a line, El Arish–Kossaima, across the approach to the Suez Canal.

During Murray's advance on Palestine, good news came from the south: the Arabs led by Husein, the Grand Sherif of Mecca, had revolted against the Turks in the Hejaz, Arabia, on June 5. The Turkish garrison at Medina was attacked that day; by the tenth Mecca surrendered to the Arabs, bolstered by Egyptian artillery. In September the Turks lost Taif. On October 29, Husein proclaimed himself King of the Hejaz and of Arabia. He had been talked into the revolt by the British with the promise of Arabian independence (with a few reservations).

A heavy German mortar on the Russian front, 1916.

Encouraged by the initial Arabian successes, the British sent Ronald Storrs (later Sir Ronald) to investigate the situation on the scene in October. He was accompanied by a decidedly unmilitary scholar-archeologist (who spoke the languages of the desert), T. E. Lawrence. He meant trouble for the Turks and for the British High Command in the Middle East as well.

The Turks were engaged also in another far-flung front, the Caucasus, where under the intelligent generalship of Nikolai Yudenich the Russians gained some ground, if no decisions. Expecting to face Turkish troops, present since the evacuation of Gallipoli, Yudenich loosed an unexpected winter campaign in mid-January, catching the Turkish Third Army off guard. Although he had taken the weather into account, the conditions were so severe that Yudenich lost an entire Don Cossack infantry battalion, which froze to death in a blizzard.

But the Russians captured Erzerum, to which the Turkish troops had retreated, on February 16. The demoralized Turks, frostbitten, and out-fought by the Russians, not only fled from Yudenich's Caucasians but also deserted in droves. The Russians pressed on and took Trebizond,

140

on the Black Sea, thus gaining an important supply port (if Czar Nicholas proved astute enough to exploit it in what he regarded a third-rate battleground). After regrouping, Yudenich began moving again in July, striking at Bayburt and reaching an important crossroads, smashing the Turkish line in half, at Erzincan. As Yudenich was short of supplies, his victorious offensive ran out of steam.

So did an attempt by a small Russian force, under General N. N. Baratov, to divert Turkish pressures on the British in Mesopotamia by moving toward Baghdad via Hamadan and Karind, which he took in March. Though this had the effect of drawing the Turkish Sixth Army away from Kut-el-Amara, it was little aid to the British garrison there. The Turks held the Russians at Khanikin in July, stopping Baratov's drive and Russian operations in neutral Persia.

When 1916 closed, the Middle East merely flickered; there was a little smoke but no real flame. It served to occupy man with the "art" of war, killing them in less dramatic numbers than on the Western Front. But those who died were just as dead, wherever they were.

On the Italian front there was sufficient bloodletting to please the most die-hard attritionist. The Italian commander, General Luigi Cadorna has been called "the out-and-out attritionist of the war" by mili-

Russian prisoners of war, trailing their own machine guns, marching into captivity.

Bulgarian infantry near Monastir, from which they were driven by Serbian and French troops in November—despite their German machine guns, which usually ruled the battlefield.

tary historian Cyril Falls. His tactic was to send his troops pounding up against Austrian positions again and again. (On the Italian right flank these charges up craggy, nearly vertical terrain produced a series of fruitless battles on the Isonzo River.) Although Italy was a latecomer to the war, in its first year, from May to December of 1915, 250,000 Italians were lost in battering away on the Isonzo in the east and the Trentino region in the west.

Although no excessive attritionist, Conrad hated his Italian foes and hoped, in 1916, to eliminate them from the war. Falkenhayn, embroiled in Verdun, refused to co-operate, so Conrad decided to do it on his own; he even managed by subterfuge to "borrow" some divisions from the Eastern Front to reinforce his armies facing the Italians.

The Italian front was a lumpy bulge, its irregular shape determined by mountains. In the east, beginning at the Adriatic Sea, it ran northward along the Isonzo, then turned westward roughly along the Carnic Alps, continuing to curve southward through the province of Tyrol, roughly to Rovereto in the Trentino. The country was razor-backed with mountains, crosshatched by rivers, and cursed with cruel, unpredictable weather.

Cadorna moved first, striking on the Isonzo in March, but with the usual gain: very little. This was called the Fifth Battle. Conrad struck next in the southern Trentino on the other end of the line. Delayed by snow, he finally ordered the Archduke Eugen (commanding a two-army group consisting of fifteen divisions) to attack. The preparations had not gone unnoticed by Cadorna, although he only had six divisions (and two in reserve) facing the Austrians.

The Austrians soon overran the Italian lines and pushed five miles into the Asiago plateau. Cadorna naturally responded by throwing in all possible reserves. By June 10 the Trentino offensive had all but come to a halt. The front had widened, creating problems of co-ordination of the Austrian Third and Eleventh armies as well as supply problems. Also, there was the distraction of the Brusilov Offensive to preoccupy Conrad.

Cadorna, with reinforcements, launched a massive counteroffensive on June 16. By the end of the month the Austrians abandoned most of their gains, moved back to prepared defensive positions, and, despite numerous Italian prisoners, guns, food, and other "spoils of war," Conrad had little more to contemplate than the fact that, in the Trentino, they were back practically where they had started.

Back then to the Isonzo, where Cadorna initiated the Sixth Battle on August 6, with a superiority over the Austrians in men and guns. On the ninth the Italians had fought their way across the river and taken a bridgehead, the fortress city of Gorizia; with this success Cadorna pushed his luck a little further and secured some footing on the Carso Plateau. His offensive declined, although he exploited these positions for his Seventh, Eighth, and Ninth Battles of the Isonzo (the last that year: November 1–14) with no further gains.

But by the time winter came, closing the campaigns on the Italian front, the cost of these battles came home: the Austrians lost about 260,000 men and the Italians close to a half million. General Franz Conrad von Hötzendorf was deposed. Italian Prime Minister Antonio Salandra, his government crumbling under the outcries over the heavy casualties, resigned. Though a little shaken, Cadorna survived—he had other battles of the Isonzo to fight and a great disaster in his future.

143

The story of the war at sea in 1916 is dominated by the controversial Battle of Jutland, the single Great Naval Battle of the war. Admiral Reinhard Scheer, recently appointed commander of the German High Seas Fleet, set off the battle when he successfully lured the British Grand Fleet into the North Sea, hoping he could wear away British naval superiority in isolated encounters.

Toward the end of May the British, thanks to the German code book that had been presented to them by the Russians, were aware of impending activity by the High Seas Fleet. There was an increase in U-boat radio activity in the vicinity of British ports. Scheer's plan was to lure the British ships within range of his main fleet; this phase of the battle began when he ordered Admiral Franz von Hipper to proceed northward into the North Sea. Once the British had moved into the trap, Scheer planned to surprise them with the main units of the German fleet.

Meanwhile, responding to Scheer's feint, the Grand Fleet, under Admiral Sir John Jellicoe, steamed out of Scapa Flow, Scotland, while to the south, Vice Admiral Sir John Beatty and the battle cruiser fleet left Rosyth and other ports. The British enjoyed a decided superiority over Scheer's ships: 28 battleships to 22, 9 battle cruisers to 5; 8 armored cruisers to none. A total of 151 British ships versus 91 German.

The first encounter occurred in the afternoon of May 31. Having completed a sweep, Beatty turned his cruisers northward to join with Jellicoe and the main fleet. He spotted five ships of Hipper's scouting force off the Skagerrak (the wide seaway leading from the North Sea between Norway and Denmark), about sixty miles southwest of Denmark's peninsula of Jutland. Hipper turned, hoping to entice Beatty into the still-unsuspected clutches of Scheer's main body of ships. The consistently aggressive Beatty steamed ahead.

He was at a disadvantage, for his ships were clearly outlined against the western skyline; the German ships were obscured in the eastern mist. In less than an hour's exchange of intense gunfire, two of Beatty's ships were lost. The *Indefatigable* vanished in a ball of flame (there were only two survivors of the entire crew), and the *Queen Mary* detonated spectacularly—smoke spouted a thousand feet above the ship—and sank; only nine men of the crew of more than 1,250 survived. In addition several other British cruisers had been hit, including Beatty's flagship, the *Lion*. When the *Princess Royal* was hit and reported (in error) lost, Beatty with characteristic aplomb commented to his flag captain, "Chatfield, there seems to be something wrong with our bloody ships today . . ." He then ordered further pursuit of Hipper's fleet.

With the approach of dusk Beatty finally sighted Scheer's battle fleet and turned to the north toward Jellicoe and his fleet. Beatty's ships

Jutland: the Queen Mary *explodes, taking most of the crew down with it.*

bringing up the rear continued to trade fire with the German ships, several of which were hit and left burning, out of action, or with decks hardly more than a jumble of wreckage.

Thus the smaller fleets led their contenders into the range of the main fleets—a double trap. They finally met after six in the evening, with Jellicoe's Grand Fleet cutting across the path of the approaching High Seas Fleet in the classic naval maneuver of "crossing the T." Scheer's ships formed the stem and Jellicoe's the top, which would enable Jellicoe to deliver broadsides on the approaching German ships. This incidentally was more by accident than design, for Jellicoe's movement toward the German fleets was plagued by small errors and communications problems (and at times no communication at all).

The battle began but Scheer brilliantly uncrossed the T with a sudden course reversal, turning his entire fleet as one ship away from Jellicoe's guns. The British battle cruiser *Invincible* soon joined its sister ships on the bottom of the North Sea. Scheer had, in his maneuvering, turned away from his home ports and the safety of their minefields. Jellicoe shifted course to head him off, but found that the German ships had been enveloped by the evening mist.

145

The "Q" turret of Beatty's flagship Lion *under repair after the Battle of Jutland.*

Neither quite knew where the other was. Then suddenly a half hour later Scheer, who had again turned to the north, appeared opposite the center of the British fleet. Firing torpedoes, he executed another wholesale reversal and faded away again into the mists. Jellicoe, in turning away from the torpedoes, also turned away from the German fleet. Night fell and Jellicoe cautiously waited.

In the night the smaller fleets exchanged volleys, both sides losing men and ships, but the main battle was over by the morning of June 1. As Jellicoe steamed south, hoping to cut off Scheer, he, in turn, headed east toward the safety of German ports. Jellicoe ordered his ships back to Scapa Flow, Cromarty, and Rosyth.

Both sides claimed a victory in the Battle of Jutland, which neither had, in fact, won. The Germans could claim a moral victory: they had held their own against the most professional navy on the high seas, had sunk more ships (fourteen British to eleven German), and suffered fewer casualties (6,784 British to 3,039 German). The British could claim that they had driven the Germans out of the North Sea—and the High Seas Fleet would remain generally bottled up in German ports for the rest of the war. Britannia continued to rule the waves. (A half century later armchair admirals continued to argue that Jellicoe might have achieved a decisive victory had he been less cautious, more aggressive like Beatty; whatever the merits of that argument, Beatty did replace Jellicoe as commander of the Grand Fleet in November.)

146

After Jutland there was no major sea battle for the duration of the war. There was a heightening in the submarine war and the loss in British and Allied tonnage rose alarmingly; so did that of the neutrals.

—◦◦◦—

The war in the air came of age in 1916; tactically it took a turn for the worse. What had once been regarded as the playboy's plaything evolved into a deadly weapon. Instead of serving merely as a flying observation platform, the flying machine, equipped with machine guns and bomb racks, emerged as an aerial gun platform or a form of winged artillery (i.e., the bomber).

A romantic folklore grew around the youthful pilots, especially in the fighter planes, whose jousting in the air evoked the imagery of knighthood. Aircraft fought over the battlefields of Verdun and the Somme, and the deeds of the airmen provided good copy for newsmen. Noncombatants became familiar with such names as Max Immelmann and Oswald Boelcke (both of whom were killed in the air, the former when his plane disintegrated and the latter when one of his students collided with him). One of Boelcke's students, a former bomber pilot, was little known in 1916, when he shot down his first British plane. He was Manfred von Richthofen, who would later be celebrated as the "Red Knight of Germany."

French and British aces were given much attention (though the British tended to be reticent at first about exploiting any single service). The French produced several individualists, among them Jean Marie Navarre (who loved to chase Parisian gendarmes on sidewalks with his auto), and Charles Nungesser, the oft-wounded ex-boxer who had achieved twenty-one victories in the air by the end of 1916 (he survived the war but died in 1927 attempting to fly the Atlantic). Georges Guynemer, the French star, had downed twenty-five German aircraft, many over Verdun, by the end of the year and was France's leading war hero.

A strangely assorted group of idealists helped to feed tales of aerial derring-do to America with their exploits in what was eventually called the Lafayette Escadrille. All were Americans who wished to fight for France; their propaganda value in the United States was incalculable. The idea for such an all-American squadron originated with Norman Prince of Prides Crossing, Massachusetts. The membership ranged from wealthy sportsmen (William Thaw of Pittsburgh) to a con-man, Bert Hall.

Among the British aces to star momentarily over the Western Front was Albert Ball; another was Lanoe Hawker (who was shot down by Richthofen). Still another, though not yet well known in 1916, was Edward "Mick" Mannock, who, despite vision in only one eye, shot down more enemy aircraft (seventy-three) than any other British pilot.

"The Monsters of the Purple Twilight," bomb-laden airships, continued to menace Britons, with continued minimal results. In the twenty-two raids of the year, many Zeppelins were forced to turn back because of weather, dropped bombs wide of the mark, and killed and injured many civilians. Some of the marauders were lost—because of anti-aircraft fire, accident, or aircraft attack.

A spectacular event was witnessed by Londoners during the great combined German Army-Navy raid the night of September 2–3, when a dozen airships attacked in a wide area around London. Second Lieutenant W. Leefe Robinson, piloting a creaky old B.E.2 (the infamous "Quirk") moved in on the giant SL-11 (a Schutte-Lanz airship, not a Zeppelin) and set it aflame in full view of the London spectators. The airship toll that night was sixteen casualties, of whom four died—but the entire crew of the SL-11, sixteen men, perished in the flaming airship. This marked the last time an Army airship raided England.

Etablissement Cinématographique des Armées

*Jean Marie Navarre, French fighter ace whose hobby
was chasing French policemen with his fast automobile.
He was killed after the war attempting to fly
a plane through the Arc de Triomphe.*

British ace Albert Ball, the first English air celebrity of the war.
He achieved his victories by headlong attack. He was twenty when
he shot down his first enemy plane in 1916. He died a year later,
with a total of forty-four planes to his credit.

In October further handwriting appeared on the wall when Germany lost its most skilled airship commander, Captain Heinrich Mathy, shot down during a raid by pilot W. J. Tempest. To escape the flames, Mathy jumped from the L-31. "With him," one of his colleagues sadly observed, "the life and soul of our airship service went out too." Perhaps, but the raids, costly and ineffectual, continued on into the final year of the war.

Other events in Britain rounded out the war year 1916. In Dublin rebels began an uprising on Easter Sunday (April 23), their objective being immediate Irish independence from Britain. The aid from Germany they had counted on never came, and by the twenty-ninth the Easter Rebellion had been put down by the British Army, its leaders killed or jailed. One of them, Sir Roger Casement (who had been slipped ashore by a German U-boat after a recruiting visit to Germany among Irish prisoners of war), was hanged that August at the Tower of London. The rebellion not only distracted the British from the war on its various fronts, but also aroused anti-British sentiment in the United States.

More directly connected with the conduct of the war was the unexpected fate of Lord Kitchener. With the persistent bad news from the

149

Pilot W. J. Tempest, who shot down the L-31 carrying Germany's supreme airship commander, Captain Heinrich Mathy.

Western Front, he managed to hold his own in the War Office, although tenuously. When his friend Nicholas II invited him to visit Russia to view the fighting there firsthand, Kitchener accepted gratefully. He no doubt looked forward to getting away from the Cabinet and all the internal quarrels. Following a brief visit with Jellicoe, who gave Kitchener a firsthand report of the Battle of Jutland, the Secretary of State for War boarded a cruiser, the *Hampshire*. Barely out of Scapa Flow, the *Hampshire* struck a mine sown by the U-75, turned over, and sank. Only twelve men survived the sinking; Kitchener was not one of them. (He was replaced as Secretary of State for War by the Minister of Munitions, David Lloyd George, who quickly learned that the office was really dominated by General Sir William Robertson, the Chief of the Imperial General Staff. The power skirmishes that followed Lloyd George's appointment convinced him that he was "out of sympathy with the spirit of the war direction. I feel we cannot win on these lines.")

Lloyd George's powerful personality—unpopular, detested, distrusted—eventually prevailed. He moved upstairs by the end of the year. Following the resignation of Asquith as Prime Minister on December 5, Lloyd George took over his duties on the tenth. Few generals were overjoyed with this hard news.

150

There were even hints and feelers for peace. Germany admitted it was ready for a negotiated peace (a peace note was issued only two days after Lloyd George became Prime Minister), although the terms were all in the Kaiser's favor. By the end of the year word had come from the tough P.M. that the note had been rejected.

In the United States, still neutral, but with men training in a few army camps, Woodrow Wilson was re-elected that November. He had "kept us out of war," as promised, but Wilson too was concerned with peace. The war encroached on American waters. This was exemplified by the U-53, which crossed the Atlantic early in October, refueled at Newport, and put out to sea again in search of British warships hunting the cargo submarine *Deutschland*. Though informed by the Americans that his quarry had left for other waters, the submarine commander, Hans

National Archives

Confronting the "enemy." Prime Minister Lloyd George, who distrusted the military and vice versa, listens with obvious skepticism to British commander Haig, while an ally, Joffre (now Marshal of France), assists. Bearded gentleman to the left is Albert Thomas, French Minister of Armaments.

Rose, decided to cruise the Atlantic outside the U.S. territorial limits. Before returning to his German base, Rose sank three British merchant ships, one Dutch, and one Norwegian just off the coast of Massachusetts.

This was disturbing to American sympathies perhaps even more than the crushing of the Easter Rebellion. Wilson, then campaigning for re-election, sent a stiff warning to the German Ambassador. After his re-election, even as the German negotiated peace feeler was being studied by Lloyd George, Wilson prepared his suggestion for an honorable "peace without victory." His proposals were rejected by both belligerents. The war would grind on.

The hard fact of 1916 was that, when the year of attrition closed, the attrition itself continued. The two all but exhausted combatants were stalemated; neither could subdue the other without fresh blood. In 1916 the Great War cracked in two, like a seesaw snapped at the fulcrum. Both ends were down and the party at either end had little control over the other. Neither wished to lose, but neither was capable of winning.

The new year held promise for nothing but more killing in the mud.

National Archives

High level conference: Joffre, the President of France Raymond Poincaré, King George V, Foch, and Haig. The last two appear not to see eye to eye. Even so, Foch talked Haig into what was to become the Battle of the Somme.

Verdun: interior of Saint-Sauveur Church.

*A German observation post at Verdun; from this point
Fort Douaumont could be easily observed.*

*Fort Douaumont, Verdun, after it had fallen to the Germans.
Crosses mark where men died during the fighting.*

Spoilage of war: a destroyed church at Voormezeele in the Ypres salient.

British reinforcements, wearing the newly issued steel helmet, arriving in France in time for the Battle of the Somme.

A big German shell tips a water reservoir, Ypres, Belgium.

THE WRONG SIDE

THOSE SHELLS THAT YOU SAW LYING IN THE MUD ARE ON THE WRONG SIDE.

PICK THEM UP

IF YOU CAN'T USE THEM YOURSELF TAKE THEM TO A

SALVAGE DUMP.

THEY WILL SEE THAT THEY REACH THE RIGHT PEOPLE WHO WILL PUT THEM IN THEIR PROPER PLACE

THE OTHER SIDE

British sign near Ypres advising troops to retrieve unexploded shells for delivery back to the Germans. The British suffered from an ammunition shortage in 1916.

An officer gingerly examines a large German shell that fell into Ypres. These were not necessarily duds and could be dangerous to inexperienced handlers—and civilians.

Ypres's historic Cloth Hall; the city, before the war, was a major cloth-producing center. The Germans never succeeded in taking it, but the town was totally destroyed in the four years of fighting around it.

Field Marshal Haig with Nicholas, King of Montenegro (whose kingdom had recently been overrun and occupied by the Austrian and German armies). Haig hoped for a quick, decisive victory on the Somme.

National Archives

A British motorized machine-gun battery behind the lines in the Somme battle zone. Little is known as to how effective this weapon was.

British forward listening post in a shell hole.

Imperial War Museu

Ready and waiting—the field headquarters of General Fritz von Below, commander of the German Second Army on the Somme. Soldiers adjust a range finder as, lower right, a message center is in readiness.

Imperial War Museum

*Over the top; a still from a motion picture filmed during the
Battle of the Somme.*

*Members of the 16th Middlesex Regiment of the 29th Division
preparing for an attack at Beaumont-Hamel. Only recently returned
from Gallipoli, they would suffer severe casualties.*

Imperial War Museu

A charge into No Man's Land. The ground had not yet been churned up by shell fire in this sector.

French Embassy Press & Information Division

An overrun German position on the Somme; artillery has had some effect. Several "potato masher" German hand grenades have been abandoned.

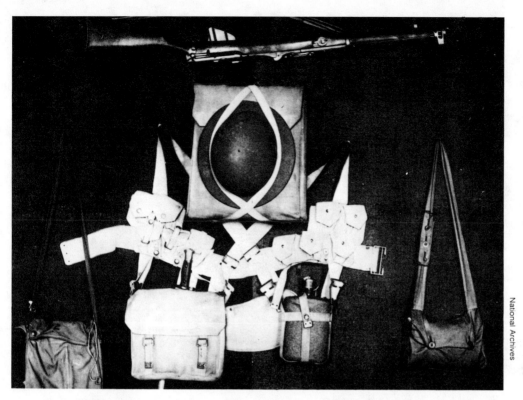

National Archives

"... burdened down with 66 pounds of equipment ..." Typical British soldier's gear carried into battle: rifle, pack and helmet, cartridge belt, canteen, gas mask, sword, and assorted carrying cases.

French Embassy Press & Information Division

The Somme battlefield takes form; French troops trailed by an ambulance head for the front.

Back from the front: Scots Highlanders march to the rear for a rest
after time in the lines. A wounded German prisoner is wheeled to a
first-aid station. The Highland Light Infantry took a German trench line
soon after the attack on the Somme began; machine guns beyond them
wiped out half of their company.

British troops dug in at Thiepval. Here the 36th Ulster Division captured the
Schwaben Redoubt and might have continued forward, but Haig forbade his senior
officers from accompanying the first attack waves. The men dug in and waited
for further orders while the Germans recovered and prepared for a counterattack.

*Where are we? British troops holding a section of nowhere,
near Martinpuich on the Somme.*

*A German trench-gun crew on the Somme; any hint of Allied
activity brought instant shelling.*

"Well if you knows of a better 'ole, go to it." The acerbic cartoons of a British officer, Bruce Bairnsfather, very accurately captured the point of view of the ordinary soldier in the front lines.

While some of his trenchmates get a little rest, perhaps after a night of heavy bombardments when sleep was impossible, a rifleman keeps an eye out for a German marauding party.

*The killer on the Somme, the machine gun. Near Ovillers,
a British crew wearing special gas masks is ready.*

*The introduction of a new weapon, the "tank." This is a Mark I,
near Thiepval on the Somme, September 1916. The first appearance of this
monster decidedly shook up German troops. But its use too soon and
in too small numbers lessened its impact later.*

*A wounded machine gunner is picked up by an ambulance for
transfer to a hospital. Rain has made the Somme earth
one of the horrors of war.*

The Somme, pastoral scene.

French troops on the Somme resting after taking a German position. Two Germans lie in the foreground.

Somme harvest: a destroyed German machine-gun position.

Somme harvest: winter mud and a long-neglected dead German.

German troops on the Eastern Front, in Galicia on the Vistula River.

Motor transport on the Eastern Front; the German troops wear an early form of helmet.

General Sir Archibald Murray who was sent to the Middle East to prevent the Turks from taking the Suez Canal; his success encouraged him to advance into Palestine.

The German High Seas Fleet in the North Sea, where Scheer hoped to lure the Grand Fleet to its destruction.

Admiral Sir John Jellicoe, commander of the Royal Navy's Grand Fleet.

Admiral Reinhard Scheer, commander of the German High Seas Fleet.

British battleships at sea, 1916.

Jellicoe springs into action as he heads for the bridge of his flagship, HMS Iron Duke.

The cruiser Invincible, *after several explosions, broke in two; there were only six survivors of a crew of 1,026. The destroyer* Badger *(right) races for a raft carrying some of the survivors.*

Jutland: Beatty's flagship, HMS Lion, *has been hit by German guns.*

A Zeppelin-built Staaken R-IV, built in 1916 and later used on both the Western and Eastern fronts. The bomber was more than 76 feet long, wings 138 feet 5½ inches from tip to tip. Its seven machine guns made it one of the most heavily armed aircraft of the war. Two gunners cover the vulnerable tail.

A German Albatros D-II, one of the more formidable fighter aircraft that came into use during 1916.

Charles Nungesser, who survived many aerial combats but not one attempt to cross the Atlantic by air.

The Lafayette Escadrille, in assorted uniforms, at Luxeuil-les-Bains, where they began combat operations during the fighting at Verdun. They are (left to right): Kiffin Rockwell; the commander Captain George Thenault (in front of William Thaw); Norman Prince; second-in-command Lieutenant Alfred de Laage de Meux; Elliot Cowdin; Bert Hall; James McConnell; and Victor Chapman.

Nieuport fighters of the Lafayette Escadrille at their base at Cachy, near the Somme.

*Lieutenant W. Leefe Robinson,
who flamed a German
airship over London.*

*A "Quirk," the type of plane in which Leefe Robinson shot down
a Zeppelin. This obsolete plane could not have survived over
the Western Front but was a serious Zeppelin contender.*

London under Zeppelin attack during daylight. The bombs have a random pattern.

Damage to a London building by a Zeppelin raid; the city was a target of minimal military value.

Antiaircraft gun with observer (left, with binoculars) and man with range finder at the right.

Commander of the German Naval Airship
Service, Peter Strasser. Leader of several
raids on England throughout the war,
Strasser was shot down in 1918.

Imperial War Museum

Star of the German Naval
Airship Service, Heinrich Mathy,
who jumped to his death
from the flaming L-31, shot
down by W. J. Tempest.

U.S. Air Force

Wreckage of the German Army LZ-77, which fell in flames near Revigny,
France, early in 1916.

The skeleton of the Zeppelin L-33, shot down near Colchester after a London raid in September 1916. Twenty-two prisoners were taken.

Prime Minister Lloyd George (partially hidden by girder) and Foreign Secretary Arthur Balfour, with others, inspect the remains of the L-32, shot down by aircraft along with the L-33. All twenty-two of the L-32's crew died.

1917

"Over There!"

THE FRENCH, in the person of the forceful, overweening General
Robert Nivelle, continued to dominate Allied strategy in the west.
When the year began, Nivelle had a plan, but, unlike the phlegmatic
Joffre, his predecessor, he had a tendency to talk about it. The plan was
to mount a great offensive in the Champagne sector (at the southern
flank of the bothersome Noyon bulge). With assistance from the British
on the Somme, Nivelle intended to use a battering ram of a million men
to drive through the German lines and end the war.

Haig, a Field Marshal since January, had his doubts; besides, he had
his own plan—an assault in Flanders. But Nivelle prevailed, even con-
vincing the canny Lloyd George that it was possible to bring the war to
a speedy close with one savage and weighty attack. The date he selected
for the new offensive was April 1. Haig reluctantly went along as Nivelle
busily made preparations. Since the plans for Nivelle's great offensive
had become widely known, it was hardly a secret to the Germans.

The Germans made two decisions early in 1917: one upset Nivelle's
brave new plan and the other indirectly settled the outcome of the war.
On January 31 it was announced that, beginning in February, Germany
would carry on a policy of unrestricted submarine warfare, a policy
forced by the success of the British naval blockade. The German people
were on a near starvation diet and suffering other shortages. Unleashing
the U-boats would soon settle the question of America's neutrality.

It was Ludendorff who upset Nivelle's plan (although the optimistic
Frenchman would not admit it) by a surprise move. From Arras in the
north to just a little east of Soissons in the south the Germans withdrew
to elaborate defensive positions along what they called the Siegfried
Line—the Allies named it the Hindenburg Line. This spoiled Nivelle's
plan to squeeze the Noyon bulge. In moving back (sometimes as much

as thirty miles), the Germans committed one of the great atrocities of the war, "Operation Alberich" (named for a destructive dwarf of German folklore). Systematically trees were cut, orchards destroyed, wells poisoned, roads dug up, railroads and bridges blown up and dwellings wrecked. And this devastation was, in turn, seeded with booby traps. The Germans left a wasteland in their wake.

By April 5 the Germans, their front constricted, were firmly stationed in the formidable Hindenburg Line. Nivelle saw this withdrawal as a move in the Allies' favor and insisted that there would be "no fundamental change whatever in the general plan of operations which have been drawn up." This could only have comforted Ludendorff and Hindenburg. So did the word from Russia, where strikes and demonstrations led to the Czar's abdication on March 15 with the words "May God help Russia."

Nothing wasted. German work crews removing metals and other valuable materials from one of the towns in the path of Operation Alberich, for removal to the Siegfried Line.

1 9 1 7

ABDICATION OF THE CZAR
KERENSKI TAKES OVER
BOLSHEVIK REVOLUTION

PERSIAN GULF

PERSIA

Basra
Kut-el-Amara
MAUDE
Diyala
Tikrit
Baghdad
TIGRIS
Ramadi
MESOPOTAMIA
Tabriz
EUPHRATES
LAWRENCE AND ARABS HARASS TURKS
ARABIA
SYRIA
1918
Megiddo
Jerusalem 1917
Jaffa
Gaza
Beersheba
ALLENBY
PALESTINE
SUEZ CANAL
CYPRUS
EGYPT

CASPIAN SEA

Tiflis

T U R K E Y

Trebizond
Bayburt
Angora
Constantinople
Smyrna
BLACK SEA

VOLGA
DON
OKA
Rostov

R U S S I A

Moscow

OCCUPATION LINE
TREATY OF
BREST-LITOVSK
MAR. 1918

ARMISTICE LINE

Kiev
DNIEPER
BUG
Odessa
DNIESTER
BESSARABIA
PRUT
KERENSKY OFFENSIVE
MOLDAVIA

Pinsk
Brest-Litovsk
Lemberg
TRANSYLVANIA
WALLACHIA
Bucharest
RUMANIA
1918
DOBRUJA

Riga
EIGHTH

BALTIC SEA
Warsaw
VISTULA

Berlin

DANUBE
SAVA
Belgrade
SERBIA
Sofia
BULGARIA
Adrianople
Monastir
ALBANIA
Salonika
(SERB.-FR.-BR.)
(IT. SERB.-FR.-BR.)
GREECE
Athens
CRETE

SWEDEN

DENMARK
Kiel
Hamburg
Bremen

NETHERLANDS
BELGIUM
LUX.

GERMANY
HINDENBURG
HINDENBURG LINE

RHINE

LINE OF NOV. 1918
AFTER BATTLE OF
VITTORIO VENETO

Vienna
AUSTRIA-HUNGARY
ELEVENTH
TENTH
SIXTH
FIFTH
Caporetto
ISONZO
TRENTINO
Vittorio Veneto
Venice
PIAVE
PO

MONTENEGRO
ADRIATIC SEA

ITALY
Rome

NORTH SEA

GREAT BRITAIN
Liverpool
London

IRELAND

ENGLISH CHANNEL
Cherbourg
Brest
A.E.F. ARRIVES

Ypres
Arras
B.E.F.
Noyon
Cambrai
ST. MIHIEL
Verdun
MARNE FR.
SEINE
Paris

FRANCE
Lyon
LOIRE
RHONE
Marseille
Bordeaux
GARONNE
BAY OF BISCAY

SPAIN

CORSICA
SARDINIA

MEDITERRANEAN SEA

SICILY
MALTA

Tunis
TUNISIA
LIBYA

Algiers
ALGERIA

N
E
S
W

MILES 400
KM 400
0

palladios

*President Woodrow Wilson announcing the severance of diplomatic relations
with Germany. In April 1917 the United States declared war.*

But there was no comfort when the United States, goaded by a stupid
diplomatic gaff and the German U-boat depredations, declared war on
Germany on April 6. Shortly after the Kaiser sent a secret message to
his navy ordering unrestricted submarine warfare, the British intercepted another message, from the newly appointed German Foreign
Minister, Arthur Zimmermann, to the German Ambassador in Mexico
City.

Zimmermann expressed the hope that America would remain neutral,
but, if not, he proposed an alliance with Mexico. In return Germany
would stand behind Mexico when it reconquered "the lost territory in
Texas, New Mexico, and Arizona." This blunder plus the American
losses to submarines prompted Wilson to demand that the "world must
be made safe for democracy," and the unprepared Americans went
cheering off to war.

180

They could not possibly arrive before the opening of the spring offensive on the Western Front, which began with a British attack at Arras, at the northern end of the Hindenburg Line, on April 9. This was supposed to draw the Germans away from the Champagne sector, where Nivelle was poised and ready.

The attack by the British was made in a blinding snowstorm, one of the final furies in what had been one of the worst winters in European history. The major effort fell to General Edmund Allenby's Third Army, and, in the beginning, all went very well. Attacking across a roughly fourteen-mile front, Allenby's troops broke the German defenses and his Canadian XVII Corps took the high ground of Vimy Ridge, which had proved so unattainable to the French in 1915. Weather permitting, planes of the Royal Flying Corps flew patrols and countered Richthofen's famed "Flying Circus" over the battleground.

Figurehead and staff: Hindenburg (boots and sword), who fronted for his Quartermaster General Ludendorff (not shown), had a grand plan for one final spring offensive and the destruction of the British Army, as 1917 came to a sorry close.

But the initial gains could not be exploited, and of course German resistance stiffened as reinforcements hardened the front. The British continued to batter against this front at various points, and by May 27 small gains had been made all along the line—the deepest penetration being about five miles from Arras. The British had to be content with that, for exhaustion took its toll and the battle could not be sustained. This was especially disheartening when it was realized that little of value besides Vimy Ridge had been gained at the cost to the British of 150,000 men (the German losses totaled about 100,000; of these more than 20,000 were taken as prisoners).

A week after the British began their costly diversion at Arras, Nivelle had his turn. He had defended his offensive against all doubters, which included his own military advisers. Nivelle silenced them with threats of resignation. The Champagne offensive—the Second Battle of the Aisne—began on April 16. As at Arras, the weather was miserable: sleet, rain, and snow resulting in mud.

Emboldened by Nivelle's certainty that the war would be over in forty-eight hours, the French troops charged over the top with much the same exhilaration they had displayed in 1914. But the French artillery barrage had failed to clean out the barbed wire and the network of machine-gun nests which "sprinkled death unhindered, as with a watering can . . ." The tanks that were to have supported the infantry arrived late and found the *poilus* exhausted from slogging in the mud. German artillery began spotting the tanks and many crews were incinerated inside. Casualties mounted and the French medical services, prepared for 15,000 wounded (and that was considered a generous number), were overwhelmed with 90,000.

But the advance that Nivelle had promised would end the war in two days ground to a halt on the first. The six miles he had expected to make shriveled to a mere 600 yards. And, although he had also promised that if the victory did not come within forty-eight hours he would call off the battle, Nivelle refused, hoping that one more day would bring victory. Attack and counterattack dragged the killing on to May 20, when both sides had had enough. The Germans were exhausted and the French mutinous. It was true, the French had advanced as deep as four miles along a sixteen-mile front and made other gains along the thirty-six-mile front that Nivelle had selected for his offensive. The Germans had suffered 163,000 casualties and more than 28,000 prisoners were taken. But the French probably lost 187,000 (the various figures are disputed).

While Nivelle had succeeded in taking back some ground, the cost had proved excessive (though hardly more than those of Joffre before him) and his vaunted conquest had not materialized. The Minister of War, Paul Painlevé, asked for his resignation (Pétain waited in the wings to assume the job of Chief of the General Staff). With charac-

182

General Robert Nivelle, whose plan to end the war in 1917 almost destroyed the French Army and led to mutiny among French troops.

Henri Philippe Pétain, hero of Verdun. In 1917 he was appointed Commander-in-Chief of the French Army.

teristic arrogance Nivelle suggested that Generals Charles Mangin and Alfred Micheler (both of whom had argued against the offensive) resign, since they were responsible for the nonvictory in the field. Micheler lost his temper and accused his superior of "cowardice."

The next day Pétain was quietly named Chief of Staff (Nivelle was shipped off to a post in North Africa), and on April 29 mutiny swept through the French armies along the front. Orders to move forward were refused, officers were beaten; in time, no fewer than fifty-four divisions were infected (the influence to some degree of an already demoralized Russian unit).

Pétain, who officially became Chief of Staff on May 15, moved into the situation with intelligence and skill. He assured the abused common soldier that better conditions would prevail—there would be leaves and rest camps, not endless days under fire. He succeeded in placating the mutinous divisions, although even an improved morale did not put the French Army in fighting trim. Pétain's favorite phrase during this parlous time was "Wait for the Americans and the tanks."

183

German trenches, Messines Ridge.

Imperial War Museum

When General John Pershing arrived in France with the first American troops in June, he was unaware of the crisis in the French Army; interestingly, the Bavarian Crown Prince heard reports of the French mutinies but—good soldier that he was—could not bring himself to take such news seriously. Had he moved on the many empty French trenches at the time, the war might have had a different history.

But the news of the French uprising was a closely guarded secret as were the courts-martial that followed—for military discipline had to be maintained if there was to be a French Army. Secrecy has blurred the facts and official reports were the least reliable. Of the 412 mutineers (out of a 100,000) condemned only twenty-three were actually executed (unofficial sources give the number as fifty-five). Some rebels were shipped to Devils Island or to penal battalions in Africa. But these disciplinary actions, serving only to save military face, were not as effective as Pétain's personal visits to nearly a hundred divisions along the front. By June all was, indeed, quiet on the Western Front. The total collapse of the French Army had been avoided, but as a fighting unit in mid-1917 it was virtually powerless.

Finally, after waiting for more than a year, Haig was to have his chance in Flanders, a thoroughly British show that possibly might have settled the war before the Yanks ever got into battle. What came to be called Third Ypres opened spectacularly at 3:10 A.M. on June 7 on the southern end of the Ypres salient. A tremendous explosion erupted

Imperial War Museum

The faces of defeat: German soldiers captured at Messines Ridge, most showing the shock produced by the gigantic mined explosion and heavy artillery shelling. The smiling man realizes that the war is over for him—and that he has, perhaps miraculously, survived.

*Wounded in the Battle of Menin Ridge, a British and a
German soldier enjoy a little peace.*

under the Messines Ridge; the shock wave was felt by Lloyd George in
London, more than a hundred miles away.

For more than a year British engineers ("sappers") had dug an elaborate system of tunnels (some as much as a hundred feet below the surface) under the German trenches. Simultaneously the Germans worked
on a similar network; like moles, enemy work parties passed one another
mere inches apart as they burrowed. Though warned, the Germans had
no idea of the complexity and extent of the British mining operations. A
million pounds of high explosives were packed into the completed
twenty-one mines. Of these, nineteen detonated simultaneously, stun-
ning even the British troops awaiting the word to attack (of the remaining two mines, one went off in July 1955, another lies quiescent under
Ploegsteert Wood).

The giant explosion was followed by an artillery barrage; German
troops suffered from above and below. The well-prepared British Second
Army, under the capable command of General Sir Herbert Plumer,
quickly overran the German front-line positions. The few stunned survivors were too numbed to surrender. Some wept, others waved handkerchiefs as a sign of surrender; some even "made many fruitless attempts
to embrace us. I have never seen men so demoralized," one British
officer later recalled.

The taking of Messines Ridge was a military, if not humane, triumph,
and Haig was more than ever determined to proceed with his Flanders
offensive. Messines had straightened out the southern end of the Ypres
salient. His objectives were the Belgian seaports Ostend and Zeebrugge,

which he insisted were U-boat nests. The success at Messines boded well. He chose to ignore the effects of heavy shelling on the earth of Flanders and upon the delicately balanced drainage system of the battle-ground. He had grand plans for his favorite branch, the cavalry. He was wrong about Ostend and Zeebrugge, too. They were not major German submarine bases—and, as the battle turned out, he never reached them.

Haig, once he had talked the War Cabinet and the Prime Minister into approving his plan, had to move quickly in order to reach his objectives before the August rains. Needless to say, the Germans from their positions were aware of the preparations; two weeks of continual artillery bombardment churned up the earth and confirmed Crown Prince Rupprecht's suspicions.

General Sir Hubert Gough's Fifth Army, too many of its nine divisions comprised of inexperienced troops, awaited the order to attack in the morning of July 31. During the evening of July 30 rain began falling.

The Germans were waiting in their machine-gun pillboxes and, behind them, reserves were poised for counterattack. Gough's men pushed forward slowly through the mud. The Fifth Army carried the main burden. To its right was Plumer's Second on the Messines Ridge, and to its left the French First Army (short of men because of mutiny-inspired leaves). Bogged down, the British reached their initial objectives only on the left of the front—and the first day's casualties amounted to nearly 32,000 men. Haig, blindingly optimistic, reported to the War Office that the day's work had been "most satisfactory."

The rains continued, and by August 4 one officer noted in his diary, "Every brook is swollen and the ground is a quagmire." Another officer touring the front (though much later) burst into tears and exclaimed,

A Mark IV tank on the Ypres battlefield.

"Good God! did we really send men to fight in that?" The junior officer accompanying him quietly replied that it was "far worse ahead."

From August until November the battle ebbed and flowed in Flanders; limited advances were followed by counterattacks. Haig had all but promised an end to the war by the end of the year. German morale, he informed his superiors, was cracking. He had also promised minimal British casualties but rationalized them with the "advances" made and claimed even greater enemy casualties. For a time in August the rain stopped, and what had once been liquid clay turned to clinging dust. The British made small gains toward Passchendaele, as Haig turned over the major thrust to Plumer's Second Army. Haig had abandoned the idea of reaching the coast and decided he would settle for a position on the Passchendaele Ridge for his winter line.

The autumn rains began on October 12; Crown Prince Rupprecht greeted it with a note in his diary: "Welcome rain, our strongest ally." If the Flanders fighting in July and August had been a nightmare, the final phase of Third Ypres, infamously known as Passchendaele, was humanly inconceivable. Men, mules, and machines frequently disappeared in a lake of mud. The main effort fell again to Gough's Fifth Army: the job of taking the site of Passchendaele—the village itself, like the rest of the Flanders landscape, no longer existed.

Canadian troops opened the battle (the eighth and final attack) on October 26, progressed slowly and on November 6 occupied the ruins of the village. By the twentieth an even sharper salient than there had been at the beginning projected into the German front. This enabled the Germans to shell from two sides the British troops occupying it. Even though Haig stated that his campaign had "served its purpose," he had,

Passchendaele: a British gun position near Langemarck. Shelling and rain have reduced the battlefield to quagmire.

". . . did we really send men to fight in that?"

in fact, failed miserably. He did not take the Belgian seaports, he did not demoralize the German troops (though they too suffered in Flanders), and he did not keep casualties to a minimum. The British losses were around 300,000 to the German's 200,000, which had a serious effect on the British soldier and the Home Front. All Haig had gotten was a final fling at staging a battle of the old style (except for one lack: he was unable to employ his beloved cavalry, because there had been no classic breakthrough and there was the mud). But the small gains had not been worth it.

He confidently looked forward to next year's big push.

During the Flanders debacle, Haig had been a bit distracted by the unhappy news from the town of Etaples, well behind the lines, near the French coast. In late September, British troops rioted and killed military police and instructors in a revolt that lasted for six days. While, unlike the French mutinies, this was not a reaction to Haig's killing spree, it was a serious warning to the British High Command. Troops en route to the battlefronts from Britain passed through the camp near Etaples for final training. The camp commander, Brigadier General Andrew Thomson, ran a tough camp. An incident ending in the shooting of an enlisted man by a military policeman led to a revolt by hundreds of British soldiers. They, in turn, hunted down MPs and "Yellow Canaries" (the drill instructors who wore yellow armbands) and beat to death as many as a dozen. In time thousands of troops joined the mutineers, who stormed the stockade and released prisoners. They also demanded a reform in the rules governing the replacement depot.

Haig, shocked by such unseemly behavior by the British fighting man, clamped a deep censorship over the events at Etaples, quickly transferred Thomson, and ordered the offenders to the front; perhaps some perished at Passchendaele. He demanded the blood of the ringleaders

189

*At the Battle of Cambrai, a tank moves forward past a number of
captured German guns. Without reserves the British could not
fully exploit their victory at Cambrai.*

(there were subsequent executions), but one, a certain Private Percy
Toplis, eluded authorities for years (he was shot by police in northern
England in 1920).

Not all the news from the Western Front in 1917 was disastrous:
Pétain had carefully restored the French Army to a fighting force and
then mounted two limited offensives. In late August the French Second
Army took some ground at Verdun with light losses; nine weeks later,
on October 23, the Tenth Army, hoping to repair some of the damage
left by the Nivelle offensive on the Aisne, eliminated the Soissons salient
and secured Fort Malmaison; a German counterattack on the twenty-
ninth failed, and a new self-confidence infused the French armies.

Even Haig had a moment of respite from the realities of Passchendaele. About fifty miles south of Ypres, on the Hindenburg Line, for the
first time in history the British launched a mass tank attack. The futile
Third Ypres had sputtered out on November 20 when, without fanfare
but under a smoke screen, more than 300 tanks smashed into a six-mile
front on the Hindenburg Line near Cambrai. The ground, unlike that at
Ypres, had been carefully selected by the commander of the Tank
Corps, General Sir Hugh Elles. Following his tanks were the infantrymen of General Sir Julian Byng's Third Army (whose previous commander, General Edmund Allenby, had been sent to the Middle East).

The two German divisions holding the line at the point of attack
crumbled, and within hours tanks and infantry overran three lines of the
German defenses. (The tanks were equipped with a device called fas-
cines, bundles of wood that could be placed over trenches and other
tank obstacles, which accounted for their speedy advance.) Only an un-

190

completed trench line stood between the Third Army and open country, but the breakout did not occur. The plan had not called for more than taking Cambrai—no one had expected so much success—and tank crews and other troops were exhausted. Worse: there were too few reserves to exploit the initial victory. The British had moved ahead about five miles in a few hours in contrast to the small gains that had taken weeks in Flanders and on the Somme.

The Germans were taken by surprise by the large number of British tanks. Only sixty-five of them were knocked out by German guns; more than a hundred simply broke down with mechanical problems. By the time British reserves were released by Haig, the Germans had time to fill the gap opened by the tanks and to bring up their own reserves. On November 30, under a barrage of gas and smoke, the Germans counterattacked and took back nearly all the ground the British had taken.

But one lesson had been driven home: the tank was a formidable weapon of war. Unfortunately for the Allies, it was a lesson that was noted more by the German than the British commanders. The tank, in conjunction with aircraft and mobilized infantry, would effectively be used against the Allies in a blitzkrieg war two decades later.

As for the Americans, who had gone to war singing the promises of "Over There!," little was heard of them during 1917. Upon arrival the green troops—"new blood" to some—were given three months of training by French veterans before being sent to a quiet sector of the front to become acquainted with the realities of trench life. The eager, bellicose Americans were informed by their French hosts, "If you see a German, don't shoot. You'll only start trouble."

"Hell," one doughboy replied, "that's what we're here for." His time would come. Units of the 1st American Division were sent to the "peaceful" Toul sector in Lorraine. Late in October the first American field artillery shell landed in the German positions; there appeared to be an increase in troop movements. The Germans became curious and on November 3 staged a raid on the American-held trenches near the village of Bathelémont, took several prisoners, and left behind the first three Americans of General John J. Pershing's American Expeditionary Forces to die on the Western Front. On November 20, when the division was relieved of front-line duty, they left an additional thirty-six dead; the 1st Division had experienced its first action at reasonable cost.

The Yanks had arrived at a time when the Allies were suffering on other fronts. Even as the Flanders battle ground on, bad news arrived from Italy. Haig had refused to release troops to be sent to Italy while he was deep in plans for Third Ypres, but Ludendorff managed to spare six German divisions for the despairing Austrians. He advised a staff officer to find a "soft spot" in the Italian line and, with the German divisions in

191

the vanguard and nine Austrian divisions following, knock Italy out of the war.

On October 24, after brief artillery preparation, the Austro-German armies burst through the Italian line at Caporetto on the Isonzo front. The Italian First Army crumbled and panicked as the Germans and Austrians poured through the breach and widened the front. Soon the Italian armies were in full retreat and by November 12, General Otto von Below had pushed some seventy miles into Italy from the Isonzo and stopped on the banks of the Piave River. The Italian defeat was a serious setback for the Allied cause and a disaster for the Italians, who lost more than 300,000 men (of which the bulk surrendered). The old warrior Cadorna was relieved and replaced by General Armando Diaz, who worked hard to hold the line and to keep demoralization from spreading throughout the Italian Army. He succeeded and in December British and French troops were sent to Italy to bolster the shaken Italians; but it had been a near thing.

Even as the Allies almost lost Italy, the final disintegration of Russia as a fighting power occurred. This began with the strange assassination of Rasputin by two Russian aristocrats in December of 1916 (he was poisoned, shot, and, still alive, dumped into the ice-covered Neva River). They feared Rasputin's hold over the Czar and Czarina and his destructive effect on Russian life. This defiant act against the Czar, as

The Italian Army breaks: deserters rushing into the Austro-German lines during the Battle of Tolmino, on the Isonzo River (and just southeast of Caporetto).

Imperial War Museum

Bolsheviks on the march, 1917. Led by Lenin, the fighting would be Russian against Russian, the Reds (Communists) vs. whatever government happened to be in power.

well as the excessive loss of Russian lives on the Eastern Front and the general discontent of the Russian people, finally erupted in the Petrograd bread riots. In March the police machine-gunned the rioters, but Russian soldiers mutinied rather than help to quell the disorders. On March 15, Nicholas II was talked into abdicating and a provisional government was established to restore order. It was challenged by the socialists, or Soviets (a council of workers, peasants, and soldiers); the more militant wing, the Bolsheviks, was led by V. I. Lenin. The Bolshevik leader, who had been living in Swiss exile, was permitted by the German General Staff to return to Russia via Germany (his railroad car was sealed while traveling through that country to avoid contact with Germans), Sweden, and Finland. The General Staff's tactic was not without merit: they hoped that Lenin would sow disaffection among the Russian soldiers. They were right.

Another exile, Leon Trotsky, heard about the disturbances at home and left New York for Petrograd. Already waiting for action was an editor of *Pravda*, Joseph V. Stalin. When the German General Staff eased Lenin back into his motherland in 1917, they had no idea what the consequences would be.

When Lenin attempted a coup in July, it failed and he fled to Finland. The tottering government was handed over to a moderate socialist, Alexander Kerensky. An attorney-orator, Kerensky talked of peace even as he urged the Russian armies to continue fighting. Brusilov was made Supreme Commander of the armies and attempted what turned out to be a final military gasp in July. There were surprising initial successes, particularly in Galicia, where an advance of twenty miles was made; but the major objective to the north, Lemberg, was not reached. The Austrians presented little resistance, but German units proved formidable. They were joined by reinforcements from the west, and on July 16 the Austro-German counterattack began. The Russian armies crumbled, and great numbers, imbued with the words of Lenin, deserted. Orders were ignored or disobeyed. Within days the Austro-Germans took back practically all of the ground won by the Brusilov Offensive of 1916.

The German Eighth Army took Riga easily on September 3. Uprisings spread throughout Russia among the peasants, workers, and the military. Kerensky was challenged by General Lavr Kornilov, who had succeeded Brusilov after the failure of the July offensive in Galicia. But Kornilov's soldier-followers deserted him on the road to Petrograd. Kerensky, his popular support dwindled, left the capital on November 7 (he later surfaced in the United States).

Lenin and Trotsky moved into the vacuum. The Bolsheviks, with the aid of the Red Guard, stormed the Winter Palace and seized the government. On November 8, Lenin issued a peace decree; an armistice was signed two weeks later. The so-called "October Revolution" (because of a calendar difference it was still October in Russia) was over. A handful of Bolsheviks had taken over all of Russia.

When peace negotiations began in early December, there was gloom in the Allied camp in the west; the German divisions, more than fifty, on the Eastern Front were released for duty on the Western Front. Ludendorff had plans for them in the spring of 1918.

The demise of Imperial Russia did not end the flow of Russian blood. After Czar Nicholas II abdicated, he and his family were kept luxuriously imprisoned by whatever government happened to be in power at the moment. In July 1918 he and his entire family were slaughtered by a local Bolshevik commander to prevent their rescue by counter-revolutionaries. In 1918 also, Trotsky headed the Russian delegation at the peace conference at Brest-Litovsk; he delayed signing the agreement so long that the Germans, irritated, began military operations again in Russia and soon convinced Trotsky of the wisdom of signing the stiffened treaty. Russia was also shaken by civil wars (beyond the scope of this narrative) that continued into the 1920s.

The fortunes of the Allies fluctuated in the more esoteric theaters of war. In the Macedonian Bird Cage, General Sarrail persisted in alienat-

Indian infantry enters Baghdad; the war in Mesopotamia is over, March 1917.

ing everyone: his unwilling hosts, the still neutral Greeks, his command (which consisted of French, British, Serbian—six divisions of each—and one Italian division), and his own high command in distant Paris. Little had occurred since the Bulgarians took Monastir in late 1916—and they were certain they could have gone even deeper into Bulgaria if Sarrail had been more helpful.

But Sarrail preferred to remain in Salonika—making threats, plans, and giving imperious orders. The Germans had rendered the front uncomfortable with the introduction of bombing aircraft. In May 1917, Sarrail attempted a general offensive, led by British General G. F. Milne, which failed because of the heavily fortified hills held by the Bulgars and a few tough German battalions, and because of the general distrust of Sarrail by the Serbs.

An even greater enemy—the anopheles mosquito—took its toll beginning each summer as entire armies were hit with malaria. A malarial soldier had little stomach for war.

Sarrail was compelled to deal with certain Greek royalist troops and was authorized to invade Thessaly. Complex military-political manipulations led to the abdication of King Constantine (suspected of pro-German sentiments, and a pro-Allied government was established with former Prime Minister Eleutherios Venizelos back in power. On July 2, 1917, Greece officially declared war on Germany, Turkey, and Bulgaria, by which time the malaria season had come and little occurred on this useless front. With a change of government in France, the new

195

Prime Minister, Georges Clemenceau, who brooked no nonsense even from the military, recalled Sarrail and in November sent General Marie Louis Guillaumat to await happenings in Macedonia.

The British enjoyed triumphs in the outer theaters, which took some of the sting out of Passchendaele. In the Egypt-Palestine battlefields General Murray attempted to take Gaza twice and failed; the second, in April 1917, was a decided defeat for the British. Murray was ordered home and Allenby, the hero of Arras and no favorite of Haig, was sent to Palestine to take over. It was July and Lloyd George's parting words contained something about being "in Jerusalem by Christmas."

Allenby devoted the first three months to preparing for such a symbolic accomplishment. He managed even to acquire a division or two from the static Salonika front and, when ready, he outnumbered the German-led Turks by about two to one. He was tendered incidental aid by the insubordinate-rebel-turned-native, T. E. Lawrence, whose exploits made him better known as Lawrence of Arabia. Leading his makeshift Arab bands, many mounted on camels, Lawrence harried the Turks by blowing bridges, wrecking ammunition and troop trains, destroying railroads, and generally spreading misery and confusion among the Turks. This helped Allenby's advance toward Jerusalem (so much that the Turks offered rewards of £20,000 for Lawrence alive and £10,000 for him dead).

When ready, Allenby began by shelling Gaza, deceiving the Turks into believing that he would take up where Murray had failed; instead, the major blow was struck inland, where on October 31 the Turkish line at Beersheba was broken. By November 6 the entire front began to crack and Allenby's troops took Gaza and fanned out onto the plain of Philistia. The deposed Falkenhayn, commanding the Turks in Palestine, attempted a counterattack at Beersheba, but the damage was done.

The British had broken through the Turkish center and, despite water shortages, pursued the two fleeing masses. Allenby continued up the coast from Gaza, reached the port city of Jaffa on November 18, then concentrated eastward toward Jerusalem. On December 9 the first British troops entered the Holy City; Allenby walked into Jerusalem on the eleventh. A Turkish attempt to regain the city on the day after Christmas failed, and the British were solidly emplaced in a line across Palestine just north of Jaffa and Jerusalem. Allenby had presented Lloyd George and the English with good Christmas tidings at a time when it was a gift indeed.

To the west and north, in Mesopotamia—yet another theater of war where politics and colonialism played as great a role as military science —the British enjoyed another symbolic victory over the crumbling Turkish Army. General Maude, who had liberated the British prisoners at Kut-el-Amara, began his spring offensive in March 1917 along the north bank of the Tigris. Ten miles below Baghdad, he slipped troops, including cavalry, across the river to the south bank over a pontoon bridge and under the cover of heavy bombardment. The Turks fell back from their strongpoint at Diyala, and on March 11 the British took the fabled city of Baghdad.

The Turkish Sixth Army, decimated by the British, disease, and hopelessness, was further weakened when reinforcements were taken from it to be sent to Palestine to counter Allenby. The small army of about 30,000 men was strung out across a wide front from the Euphrates River to the Persian border. The autumn campaign began in early November, for during the summer all that anyone could do was to plan, prepare, and avoid illness and heat prostration.

British cavalry and Indian infantry moved the line northward, up the Tigris and the Euphrates to Ramadi and Tikrit; on November 18, General Maude, who had gained the respect and affection of his men and commanders, died of cholera in Baghdad. (His successor, General W. R. Marshall, continued to batter the already battered Turks.) In Britain, only Allenby's entrance into Jerusalem lessened the gloom that the news of Maude's death had brought to Britain.

But these two symbolic victories, requiring thousands of troops that might have served more usefully elsewhere, did not in fact really "get on with the war," except for contributing to the further disintegration of the Turkish fighting spirit.

Once in Jerusalem, or in Baghdad, the British soldier could very well have asked, "Now that we are here—where are we?"

It was pretty much the same in East Africa, where the slippery Colonel Paul von Lettow-Vorbeck continued to hold out, if not win battles. A small force of South Africans, Belgians, and British (each with a stake in East African colonies) continued to pursue him through the bush, over mountains and lakes, but Lettow-Vorbeck managed to elude them—and to engage good numbers of British troops chasing around the bush. In July 1917, after the summer rains, the British began tracking him again and even succeeded in taking one of his lieutenants and some 5,000 troops, but Lettow-Vorbeck slipped across the frontier into Portuguese West Africa (Angola). He continued to elude Portuguese and British troops for the rest of the war and eventually led a small band into Northern Rhodesia. (By this time the war ended and Lettow-Vorbeck, the last holdout, finally surrendered on November 23, 1918—days after his Fatherland had capitulated.)

But "the real war" lay elsewhere, and in 1917 few expected it to end before 1919. The U-boat campaign that Germany initiated in February not only eventually brought the United States into the war but also led to serious shortages in Britain. It was also a threat to the transportation of American troops to the battlefronts. By April 1917, Britain lost one out of every four ships that put to sea; by October, it was projected, Britain could run out of ships at that rate.

The conventional methods of combating the German submarines were not effective. German minesweepers cleared the minefields that should have contained the U-boats; fitting merchant ships with guns did not always work; nor did "Q" ships, which appeared to be merchant ships but were in fact decoys whose "cabins" camouflaged a heavy gun, so that when a submarine surfaced, the sides of the cabin fell away and the battle could begin.

It was in April that American Rear Admiral William S. Sims traveled to London to confer with Jellicoe and learned that it was "impossible for us to go on with the war if losses like this continue." Sims soon allied himself with Beatty, Commander Reginald Henderson, and a group of younger officers, who favored yet another method of dealing with the submarine. This was, simply, the full employment of the convoy, which had had limited use in the past. The merchant ships crossed the Atlantic in groups escorted by armed destroyers. The American Navy was especially active in this work—which, in time, eliminated the submarine as a serious threat to the Allies.

The German people suffered too from the British blockade and the mining of seaports. The underfed German soldier at the front was further dismayed when he received letters from home complaining of food shortages. Inside Germany, 1917 was called "the year of the turnip." There was also a shortage of coal in one of the coldest winters in European history. There were mutterings of strikes, even intimations of revolution. Socialist leader Philipp Scheidemann spoke of "want, hunger and bewilderment" and even of "a peace of reconciliation." But the Hindenburg-Ludendorff combination on the Western Front would not hear of that and they formulated plans for the new year—a great offensive before the full strength of the Americans could arrive.

—⚜—

If the submarine waned by the close of 1917, military aircraft began to come into their own that year. The Zeppelin raids over London dwindled down to seven for the year (with forty-six airships participating). During the last raid of the year (October 19–20) eleven Navy airships left Germany, hoping to attack from the high altitude of 12,000 feet; because of this, their engines were not heard on the ground and this hapless mission has come to be called "The Silent Raid." At that altitude the great ships were buffeted by high winds and scattered. Although dispatched to bomb targets in the industrial Midlands, those ships that did bomb dropped them on London. Four of the airships did not return

—one being hit by French antiaircraft guns, the others damaged by high winds. Another was wrecked while landing in Germany. It had proved to be a wasteful mission: the loss of five airships (almost half of the total force) for no gain.

By this time the Germans had introduced another bomber, *Riesenflugzeug* (giant aircraft), capable of carrying heavy bombloads to England. These planes began bombing London during daylight hours in May and, because of losses to antiaircraft guns and fighter planes, switched to night bombing in August. Several types of giant aircraft were used, but the best known was the Gotha (in time all giant bombers were called Gothas). Though more destructive than the Zeppelins, the big bombers accomplished little more than scattered damage and large numbers of civilian casualties, but no panic and demands for peace.

Aces proliferated, especially over the Western Front, during 1917. So did improved aircraft, as the Allies and the Central Powers attempted to counter each improvement in design, engine, or firepower. Air superi-

U.S. Signal Corps

Crew of the submarine U-58 surrendering. Photo was taken from the deck of the USS Fanning. *American ships played a large role in Atlantic convoys, the most effective method of dealing with U-boats.*

ority on the front seesawed from one side to the other, depending on the excellence of newly introduced planes. The German Albatros D-III, for example, dominated a portion of the front in early 1917—it was the plane flown by Richthofen's Jagdstaffel 11, the' "Flying Circus," that was moved along the front to spots where it might be required. The Albatros, in turn, was challenged by the British S.E.5 and later the superior Sopwith "Camel." These planes were flown by such colorful British aces as Edward Mannock and Albert Ball, and the Canadian William Bishop.

The French ace of aces Georges Guynemer flew the tough, hard-to-handle Spad. All France mourned the sickly pilot when he was killed in September. The new ace of aces, René Paul Fonck, immediately set out to avenge the death of France's great air hero. With a total of seventy-five victories Fonck was France's—and the Allies'—highest-scoring fighter pilot.

The Americans in British or French air units also flew the Nieuport, Spad, or later the S.E.5. (The American squadrons would not see action until April 1918.) These individualists learned in 1917 that aerial tactics had changed since the war began, and ground commanders began to realize the importance of aerial reconnaissance, bombardment, formation flying, strafing, and bombing trenches and troop concentrations. Aircraft, it was grudgingly admitted, had proved effective over Arras and Ypres. Foch had been wrong when he said, in 1914, "The aircraft is very good for sport—for the army it is useless."

By 1917 it was obvious that a formidable new weapon was aborning. But its full impact would have to wait for one more war. The decisive battles of the Great War were fought on the ground, and Ludendorff had decided that, because of the situations in Russia and Italy (as well as the American threat), he would go over to the offensive on the Western Front with hammerblows that would end the war. He announced this plan to his staff, or their lieutenants, at Mons on November 11, 1917.

Within a year to the very day, Ludendorff would be proved correct in one premise of his great plan.

German propaganda poster, 1917, urging the U-boats to attack
Allied and Allied-bound shipping: "U-Boats Out!"

Hindenburg (left) indicates a point on the map for the Kaiser
while Ludendorff observes. Ludendorff's decision to constrict the German lines
and establish the Siegfried Line (the Allies called it the
Hindenburg Line) upset the Allied plans for a spring offensive.

Systematic destruction. The French town of Saint-Quentin on the Hindenburg Line. Some of the damage has, of course, been done by shellfire.

A dugout, protection from shells and air attack, near a French farmhouse that served the Germans as a headquarters in Nesle, on the Somme.

The coded Zimmermann Telegram,
of January 1917, sent over
U. S. State Department lines,
informed the German Legation in
Mexico City of the start
of unrestricted submarine warfare.
It offered to Mexico portions
of Texas, New Mexico,
and Arizona for Mexican aid
against the United States.
The message was sent in
the name of the German
Ambassador to the U.S.,
Johann-Heinrich von Bernstorff.

WESTERN UNION TELEGRAM

NEWCOMB CARLTON, PRESIDENT

CLASS OF SERVICE DESIRED
Fast Day Message
Day Letter
Night Message
Night Letter

Send the following telegram, subject to the terms
on back hereof, which are hereby agreed to

via Galveston

JAN 19 1917

GERMAN LEGATION

MEXICO CITY

130	13042	13401	8501	115	3528	416	17214	6491	11310
18147	18222	21560	10247	11518	23677	13605	3494	14936	
98092	5905	11311	10392	10371	0302	21290	5161	39695	
23571	17504	11269	18276	18101	0317	0228	17694	4473	
23284	22200	19452	21589	67893	5569	13918	8958	12137	
1333	4725	4458	5905	17166	13851	4458	17149	14471	6706
13850	12224	6929	14991	7382	15857	67893	14218	36477	
5870	17553	67893	5870	5454	16102	15217	22801	17138	
21001	17388	7446	23638	18222	6719	14331	15021	23845	
3156	23552	22096	21604	4797	9497	22464	20855	4377	
23610	18140	22260	5905	13347	20420	39689	13732	20667	
6929	5275	18507	52262	1340	22049	13339	11265	22295	
10439	14814	4178	6992	8784	7632	7357	6926	52262	11267
21100	21272	9346	9559	22464	15874	18502	18500	15857	
2188	5376	7381	98092	16127	13486	9350	9220	76036	14219
5144	2831	17920	11347	17142	11264	7667	7762	15099	9110
10482	97556	3569	3670						

BERNSTORFF.

Charge German Embassy.

The Allied spring offensive opens on the Western Front. British troops near
the Feuchy crossroads, Arras, April 1917. A line of infantry moves toward
the rear. Artillery (18-pounders) indicates the direction of the front lines.

German troops counterattack over the battered earth at Arras.

A British howitzer in action near Arras, May 1917. By this time the spring offensive had run out of steam.

Prime Minister Lloyd George views the results of master plans: the graves of the soldiers killed in battle.

*A big German gun under camouflage; this is a 38-cm. rapid-firing
weapon that made a shambles of towns and cities and
a desolation of No Man's Land.*

A 38-cm. gun in operation.

At a German outpost. This device was used to pick up the sound of enemy activity for German artillery.

Front line shock troops assemble a trench mortar. Shells from this monster could be lobbed into shell holes and even trenches where troops took shelter.

Fresh French troops on their way to the front.

Rheims Cathedral, with sandbag protection from shelling. The men in the foreground study the damage already done by German artillery fire. It was in the vicinity of Rheims, in the wake of Nivelle's offensive, that French troops began to mutiny.

A British heavy gun, pulled by a tractor, being moved into position for a barrage on German trenches.

British Tommies dug in near Menin Ridge. Third Ypres continues despite small gains and large numbers of casualties.

Third Ypres—British soldiers dig out wounded infantrymen after a direct hit by a German artillery shell.

The quality of mercy . . . stretcher-bearers carry a wounded enemy away from the Battle of Menin Ridge, September 1917.

First aid: a medic (right) administers to a wounded man, while another (himself wounded) takes down information for next of kin.

A gunner and the battery mascot, Ypres 1917. The British Army was by then conscripting the young and the old.

*Third Ypres in its final phase, Passchendaele, after the
autumn rains began.*

*Tanks on the way to Cambrai to attack the Hindenburg Line. Each carries
a fascine (a bundle of wood), which could be placed
in ditches, enabling the tank to pass over.*

The German Crown Prince observes as a crew demonstrates a flamethrower.
Generally used to drive men out of fortified positions, it was
also effective against tanks. Incineration was introduced as yet another
modern method of killing in war.

Germans dismantle one of the British tanks lost at the Battle
of Cambrai; scrap metal could be reused for munitions.

American recruiting posters designed by two of America's celebrated illustrators: James Montgomery Flagg for the Army and Howard Chandler Christy for the Navy. Flagg appealed to patriotic sentiments and Christy appealed to the male ego.

A proliferation of Navy recruiting posters. At top right, the potential enlistee is admonished not to read American history, but to make it. At bottom right, a recruit's mother turns him over to Uncle Sam.

*General John J. Pershing
was selected to lead the
American Expeditionary Force
to a warring Europe.*

*British troops study a heavy German gun captured during the
tank attack at Cambrai, November 1917.*

The "art" of war: a British sergeant instructs American soldiers in the niceties of constructing trenches at Camp Lee, Virginia.

U.S. Signal Corps

The first American troops docking at Saint-Nazaire, France, June 1917.

U.S. Signal Corps

President Wilson delivers a message to doughboys on the way to war.

American troops in London about to embark for France.

Kaiser Wilhelm in discussion with his commander in Northern Italy, General Otto von Below.

*German preparation for movement on the Russian front—a sleigh park.
This primitive method of transportation was often more efficient than
the modern truck over Russian terrain and in Russian weather.*

*The fighting virtually over, Italian refugees return to their
homes between the Brenta and Piave rivers after Caporetto.*

*A German advance against the Russians; the sleigh carries
baggage and equipment.*

Vladimir Ilyich Ulyanov, better known as Lenin, the Marxist revolutionary who played an important role in the October Revolution. As Chairman of the Council of People's Commissars, Lenin made peace with Germany.

Leon Trotsky, who returned to his native Russia from the United States for the Bolshevik Revolution.

The Russian royal family in better times. Czar Nicholas II (seated at left); he, his wife, four daughters, and son were taken into custody after his abdication in March 1917.

Revolt in Petrograd; soldiers and students fight the Russian police in the take-over of the Winter Palace. The city was later renamed Leningrad.

*Czar Nicholas, a prisoner of the state, at Tsarskoe Selo,
one of several palaces where he and his family were
detained until their murder in July 1918 by a Bolshevik
commander who feared they might be freed by counterrevolutionaries.*

General Otto Liman von Sanders (center, hand raised) on the Palestine front, 1917. Liman von Sanders was an adviser to the Turks during the Gallipoli campaign and in the final battles in Palestine.

Turkish machine gunners awaiting the approach of Allenby's troops pushing toward Jerusalem.

The legendary T. E. Lawrence, "Lawrence of Arabia," who chose to fight with the Arabs against the Turks. Leading small bands of camel-borne warriors, Lawrence harassed the Turks in Allenby's path with sudden attacks and by dynamiting railroads and bridges.

Arabs on the march; motley bands like this served under Lawrence.

Turkish soldiers at Beersheba, which was taken by Allenby's advancing troops in October 1917.

Victor in Palestine: Allenby rides up to Jerusalem's Jaffa Gate. His entry into the city, in time for Christmas, was made on foot, December 11, 1917.

Arabian Prince Faisal (foreground) and the Arabian delegation at a postwar peace conference in Paris. Lawrence (second from right) served as an adviser to the delegation. He was bitterly disappointed that the Allies' promises to the Arabs during the war were not kept; France and Britain obtained mandates in what were to have been Arab territories.

Indian transport troops in Mesopotamia on the way to Baghdad. The use of mules for hauling also required bringing in their feed.

Advance headquarters of the British I Corps, Mesopotamia. The trenches were once occupied by Turks. At far right, a signaler sends a message by heliograph. Captain Kermit Roosevelt is seated at far left.

Kermit Roosevelt, son of Theodore, serving with the Royal Engineers, wades through the Aq Su Wadi River, Mesopotamia. Roosevelt later joined the American Army in France.

Turkish civilians at Ramadi surrender to British advance troops.

Turkish troops surrendering at Tuz Khurmatli, Mesopotamia, April 1917.

Turkish prisoners, taken at the battle for Ramadi, are herded through Baghdad.

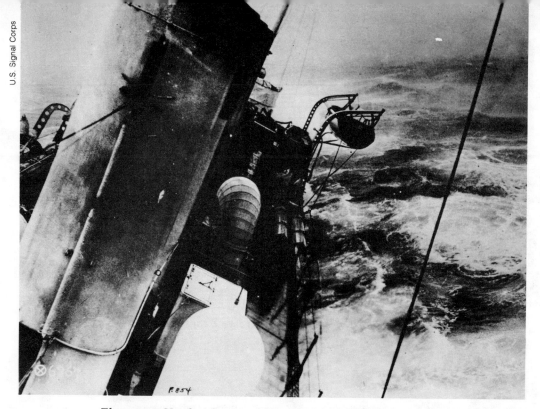

The stormy North Atlantic, major operating waters for German submarines.

Admiral Scheer, whose submarines were ordered to cripple Allied shipping and troop transport and to avenge the effective blockade of Germany.

Submarine base at Kiel, Germany. Torpedoes are being loaded aboard torpedo boats and submarines.

Another form of convoy protection: smoke screen. The USS Henderson *in battle paint lays down a layer of smoke.*

In honor of the visit of King George V, these crew members of a U. S. Navy battleship appear in uniform and black tie.

"Alas! My Poor Brother!"
The propaganda war against
the Germans took a grisly
turn in 1917 when it was
reported that they were
distilling glycerine from
the bodies of their dead.
Not until 1925 was it
learned that this tale was
invented by British military
intelligence. Cartoonist
Bairnsfather contributed
to the legend in this drawing
of a German munitions worker.

A German view of the typical
German soldier. The appeal
reads "Help Us Win!" The
poster by Fritz Erler was
used in a war loan drive.

Aerial view of London. A kite balloon used in training observers for the front hovers over the city.

Giant Gotha bombers of Heavy Bomber Squadron No. 3—the Englandgeschwader—prepare for a raid on London. The British capital was bombed by Gothas for the first time on June 13, 1917, leaving behind 162 dead and more than 400 injured. It was obvious that bomber aircraft were more "efficient" than the Zeppelins.

The grounded L-49 forced down by aircraft in France after
the fruitless "Silent Raid" of October 20, 1917. Off course
and suffering engine and radio problems—plus the attentions of
five Nieuport fighter planes—Captain Hans-Karl Gayer landed the
airship. It was later dismantled, and parts were distributed among
the Allies; the crew of nineteen was taken prisoner. The photo
taken in the pilot house shows that the ship had
nosed into a wooded area.

Close-up of another giant German bomber, the A.E.G. (Allgemeine Elektrizitäts Gesellschaft), which looked more formidable than it actually was. The Gotha was superior to the A.E.G.

Bombers, because they were heavy and slow, were often the easy targets of fighter planes. This D.F.W. C-V (Deutsche Flugzeug Werke) was shot down over France.

Raymond Collishaw (standing), third ranking British ace. A Canadian, Collishaw shot down sixty German planes and survived the war (he also served in World War II). The plane is the tough Sopwith "Camel" and the pilot is Captain A. T. Whealey.

William Bishop, also a Canadian, was the second ranking ace with seventy-two victories. He is seated in the cockpit of a French Nieuport.

The British S.E.5, one of the better Allied fighters of the closing months of the war.

The famed, rugged French Spad (Société pour Aviation et ses Dérivés). Though not an easy plane to fly, the Spad's construction held up well under air fighting and abusive pilots. It was a favorite of American fliers.

French Nieuport 28s "somewhere in France." More delicate than the S.E.5 and Spad, the Nieuport was a proven fighter plane but needed a skilled pilot. In a dive, however, it had the disconcerting tendency to lose the fabric from its upper wing.

A German observation balloon, popularly called the Drachen
*(dragon). Balloons of both sides floated over the front
lines spotting artillery fire and reporting troop movements.
Fighter pilots were dispatched to knock them down—no easy
assignment, for the balloons were ringed with antiaircraft
guns or were protected by their own aircraft.*

*Dogfight: a German plane,
disintegrating, falls into
No Man's Land on the Western
Front as the victorious S.E.5
pulls away. Actually, this
is a faked composite photo
widely circulated after the
war by a Mrs. Cockburn-Lange,
who said that a British
fighter pilot took the photos
with a camera on the upper
wing of his S.E.5. This was impossible,
since the wings of aircraft
of the period vibrated a
great deal. However, many
Cockburn-Lange photos did
capture some of the feel
of air combat.*

*The winter of our discontent: the Kaiser (saluting) and the Crown
Prince reviewing troops in December 1917. The Germans were preparing for
the final blow that would end the war in 1918.*

1918

"Where Do We Go from Here?"

BRITISH POET Edmund Blunden described the coming of the New Year on the Western Front as he and fellow soldiers observed the sky scribed by flares and star shells: "The writing on the night was as the earliest scribbling of children, meaningless; they answered none of the questions with which the watcher's eyes were painfully wide.

"Midnight; successions of coloured lights from one point, of white ones from another, bullying salutes of guns in brief bombardment, crackling of machine-guns small on the tingling air; but the sole answer to unspoken but importunate questions was the line of lights in the same relation to Flanders as at midnight a year before. All agreed that 1917 had been a sad offender. All observed that 1918 did not look promising at its birth."

Blunden and his trenchmates were agreed on another proposition: the war would go on forever. The less poetic merely referred to the Western Front as "the sausage machine" because, as explained by writer Robert Graves (who was there also), "it was fed with live men, churned out corpses, and remained firmly screwed in place."

The Allies were certain that Ludendorff would activate the sausage machine early in 1918; the Allies were aware, too, of the meaning of the Russian defection: more divisions for Ludendorff in the west. And Ludendorff knew that he would have to strike before fresh meat for the machine arrived in the form of American divisions. He planned a series of hard blows, quick and surprising. This was a technique that had worked well on the Eastern Front. It had been developed, if not conceived, by General Oskar von Hutier on the Russian front. Besides only a brief artillery barrage, it employed the tactic of bypassing strongpoints —infiltration, in other words—and moving forward quickly. This isolated the more difficult enemy units which then could be taken care of later, or by reserves, while the German vanguard pushed forward. Significantly, Hutier had been transferred from the east to lead the German Eighteenth Army, at the point where Ludendorff planned to strike his first blow.

On January 21, during a tour of the front, Ludendorff made his final decision. Although he preferred to strike in Flanders and drive the British into the sea, he realized that the weather and terrain would operate against him; instead he selected the weakest portion of the Allied line. This was held by Gough's Fifth Army, thinly strung out, facing the Hindenburg line roughly from Cambrai to the Oise River (where the

The Russian delegation, headed by Trotsky (center, with scarf), arrives in Brest-Litovsk for a peace conference with the Central Powers, December 1917. Trotsky, a great debater, delayed the signing of the treaty for weeks, hoping that the revolution fomenting in Russia would also infect Germany and Austria. He was wrong.

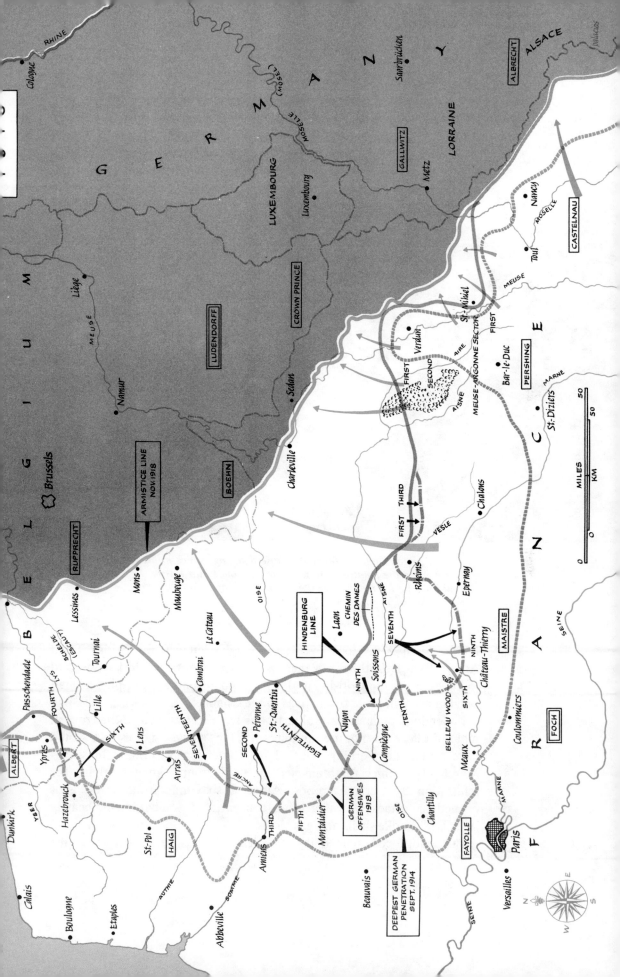

The enigmatic smile of Trotsky, whose delaying tactics infuriated the Germans to the point of resuming their advance into Russia, could not be his reaction to the harsh terms of the Treaty of Brest-Litovsk in March 1918.

French Sixth Army took over); to Gough's left was the British Third Army (Byng). In the north then, where Ludendorff would have wished to attack, were the British Third, First, and Second armies, plus a small Belgian army in place from Arras to the Channel.

Ludendorff planned carefully; troops were transported to the front at night; artillery was not used to announce the "show," and, as luck would have it, on the morning selected for Ludendorff's spring offensive— March 21—a thick fog blanketed the battleground, greatly helping the infiltration by German troops. Along a sixty-mile front 6,000 guns opened the attack; it was a brief, concentrated bombardment, heavily laden with smoke shells and gas shells.

Ludendorff code-named it "St. Michael"; it is better known as the

238

Second Battle of the Somme. And for a time it worked. Both the British Third and Fifth armies were pushed back alarmingly, particularly the latter, as infiltrators moved into the battle zone around the machine gunners unable to see because of dense fog. Within a week Hutier's Eighteenth Army was about thirty miles from Paris, a chilling echo of 1914. Parisians had already received a deadly harbinger of the German approach: on March 23 at around seven in the morning a gigantic explosion rocked the city; twenty minutes later, there was another. The first had merely caused damage; the second, which landed near the Gare de l'Est, killed eight and injured thirteen. The Germans on that day were

One of the results of the Treaty of Brest-Litovsk was the freeing of German divisions from the Eastern Front for use in Ludendorff's Operation St. Michael, his big spring offensive.

Imperial War Museum

239

more than sixty miles away and no aircraft had appeared overhead. The Germans in fact had developed a gun capable of firing a 276-pound projectile over a distance of seventy-five miles. Quite an achievement except for one problem: it was impossible to aim the gun with any accuracy. During its entire lifetime, this Krupp-built monster did not hit one military target. On Good Friday, March 29, one of its shells fell into a church, killing eighty-eight worshipers, sixty-nine of them women and three children. The "Paris Gun" would continue such random slaughter until July, to no great effect upon Parisian morale.

As the British front crumbled, the Germans advanced forty miles, taking several towns including Péronne and Montdidier, beyond which they were stopped by the arrival of French reinforcements. The surprising push ground down by April 4, when even the victors had begun to tire. There was a large bulge in the Allied line from Arras in the north to the Oise River in the south. Ludendorff, too, unwittingly contributed to the Allied cause: despite the obvious success in the south, he curbed a fuller exploitation of it in favor of pressing toward Arras further north. After the initial surprise, the British recovered and, with French aid, stopped the offensive. But the Fifth Army was a shambles and Gough became the scapegoat; he was replaced by General Sir Henry Rawlinson. Although Allied losses were high (a total of 230,000, mostly British), so were Ludendorff's. He had not succeeded in making a great breakthrough and he had begun wearing down his own troops.

German soldiers moving into territory once held by the British were astonished at the mounds of fine equipment left behind. It soon dawned on them that someone had lied to them: the submarine campaign had not been the success the High Command had claimed. The British blockade, on the other hand, had diminished German supplies, even of food. So it was that one day, on March 28, somewhere between Albert and Amiens (with its important railway junction), the German advance stopped. Since there was no enemy opposition, German officers went ahead to investigate. They found the once disciplined German soldiers looting. "Men dressed up in comic disguise. Men with top hats on their heads. Some carried useless objects such as "a silk drawing-room curtain," or "writing paper" and "colored notebooks." And many were hopelessly drunk, for they had also found ample French wine cellars.

His first hammerblow having failed, Ludendorff unleashed another, again primarily at the British. This occurred as his southern advance had begun to wind down without having decided anything. The new attack, the Lys Offensive, begun on April 9, shook Haig. The Germans struck on a narrow (twelve-mile) front south of Ypres in Flanders; their major goal was the rail center, Hazebrouck, after which they hoped to wheel northward to the Channel. A Portuguese division directly in the path of the attackers turned and ran; by the next day the Germans had

German infantry and artillery concentrations waiting in the ruins of Saint-Quentin for the opening of the Second Battle of the Somme.

widened the gap to a thirty-mile front and had thrust five miles into the British lines. The British were forced off their celebrated Messines Ridge; even Passchendaele was abandoned.

The crisis accomplished what months of argument had not: the appointment of an Allied Commander-in-Chief in France: Foch. This, it was hoped, would make for less squabbling between the British and French high commands, particularly between Haig and Pétain. Neither liked relinquishing troops to the other and each was motivated, even if subconsciously, by divergent strategies: Pétain always had the defense of

Paris in mind and Haig had his on the Channel ports, his major source of supply, and, if necessary, escape. The appointment of Foch did not solve all personal problems, but it was a step in the direction of unified command and co-ordination of effort.

Ludendorff, who had originally intended the Lys Offensive in Flanders as a diversion, was delighted with the unexpected success and continued to pour his limited supply of reserves into the crack in the line (the bulk of his reserves were busy holding the bulge on the Somme further south). The British, too, were short of reserves. Some attributed

Imperial War Museu

British field guns prepare to meet the Germans near Arras. By diffusing the force of his offensive, Ludendorff gave the Allies time to recover and to halt the spring offensive.

that to the fact that Lloyd George was loathe to release them to Haig because of the bloodletting of the year before.

On April 12 the desperation of the situation was revealed when Haig issued a Special Order of the Day, the last paragraph of which stated: "There is no course to us but to fight it out. Every position must be held to the last man; there must be no retirement. With our backs to the wall and believing in the justice of our cause each one of us must fight on to the end. The safety of our homes and the Freedom of mankind alike depend upon the conduct of each one of us at this critical moment."

By April 29, when the Battle of Lys closed, the Germans had taken the entire Ypres salient for which the British had bled so heavily in the past; they bled again losing it. The German drive was stopped because in fact it had run out of steam and Ludendorff in his enthusiasm had pushed it beyond the capacity of his troops (they never did reach Hazebrouck). Also, though reluctantly, Foch dispatched French divisions to the north to assist the British in halting the German assault. Both sides had lost heavily since the spring offensive began: more than 21,000 Allied soldiers were killed and 250,000 wounded. The German figures were even more appalling, for over 56,000 German soldiers had died, 181,000 had been wounded, and hundreds of thousands on both sides were "missing." Clearly, Ludendorff's "victories" were costly.

But he was also desperate; he had promised a smashing victory on the Western Front and had managed to expend thousands of men on two victories without any final result. And as he used up his troops, the Americans moved, as he well knew, into the battle zones. He did not know that Pershing did not fully accept Foch as the Supreme Allied Commander, nor that the American commander intended to keep his American divisions intact, as a single fighting unit, and not sacrifice them piecemeal every time Haig or Pétain cried out for reserves. When Ludendorff's spring offensive opened in March, there were eight American divisions in France (an American division was about twice the size of European divisions), some 30,000 troops. Their participation had until that time been minimal. During the Somme crisis Pershing informed Foch that the American divisions were at his disposal, though he continued to be parsimonious in releasing Americans to serve under foreign commanders. Not until May would American soldiers see action in great numbers, and by that time Ludendorff struck again.

This Third Battle of the Aisne opened on May 27 and sputtered out by June 6; Ludendorff had selected a thirty-mile front between Soissons and Rheims. The French Sixth Army was the major target as Ludendorff hoped to lure French troops away from Flanders in the north, where he had further plans for his real final blow. Taken by surprise, the French were driven back from the lightly held Chemin des Dames and pushed

243

across the Aisne River. On the first day the Germans had driven about ten miles inside the French lines. Although he reached his objective—the line along Vesle River from Soissons to Rheims—by May 28, Ludendorff was so impressed with his success that he set aside his plan for a major offensive in Flanders and ordered the attack to continue. By May 30 the German center had reached the Marne at Château-Thierry, fifty miles from Paris. The advance had by then penetrated into the French positions more than thirty miles.

Elated by his unexpected gains in Champagne, Ludendorff abandoned the Flanders idea and attempted to straighten out his line between the Somme salient and the new one on the Marne. A hastily prepared attack roughly in the center, aimed at Compiègne and generally called the Battle of the Matz, opened on June 9 and petered out by the fourteenth. The French line held and Ludendorff managed to gain a mere six useless miles.

Americans acquiring front-line experience in a "quiet" sector near Ancerville, March 1918, while Ludendorff hammered at the British and French to the north.

*Not so quiet. Americans in the Toul sector (just south of
the Saint-Mihiel salient) seek shelter from German shellfire.*

Although Ludendorff's blows had run down, there was serious cause
for alarm in the Allied camp. Because of the emergency, Pershing was
persuaded to release two American divisions, the 2nd and 3rd, to the
French. For the first time, on June 4, Americans participated in a full-
scale battle when they assisted the French in repulsing German attempts
to cross the Marne at Château-Thierry. (Americans actually went into a
sizable but local action earlier on the Somme salient when, on May 28,
the 1st Division took and held the village of Cantigny.)

The Americans were cocky, full of fight, and, unlike their trenchmates
the *poilus,* fresh and inexperienced. A Marine brigade was attached to
the 2nd Division in the vicinity of Belleau Wood and met head-on those
Germans that had been deflected from Château-Thierry by the 3rd Division in the east. The fighting was hard, and when a French officer advised Marine Colonel Wendell C. Neville (5th Marines) that the dis-
creet thing to do was retreat, Neville's reply was a characteristic,
"Retreat, hell! We just got here!" They stayed and the Germans were
driven out of Belleau Wood and other strongholds, including Vaux, by
the end of June. But American casualties were high—as high as 40 per
cent in some units—but, another but, they had destroyed four German
divisions.

The increasing American presence and the battle weariness of his own
troops appear not to have registered on Ludendorff. On July 4 it was
publicly announced that a million Americans had been transported to

245

A big German gun, the type that could fire a heavy projectile over great distance, like the infamous "Paris Gun."

France; even so, Ludendorff had plans for what he called a *Friedensturm* (peace offensive), which would enlarge his gains on the Aisne and enable him to continue on to Paris; then with this as a diversion he would finally get around to Flanders. The Allies were ready for him; forewarned by loquacious German prisoners and aerial reconnaissance, Foch assembled more than twenty French divisions, nine American, four British, and two Italian, and waited (an additional four British divisions were kept in reserve). He even knew the date set for the opening of *Friedensturm:* July 15.

When the Second Battle of the Marne opened that day, Ludendorff had already been outfoxed by Pétain, who, as Commander-in-Chief, had argued the commander of the Fourth Army to the east of Rheims into a so-called "elastic defense in depth." Instead of placing the major troop strength in the forward trenches, where they were generally cut to pieces by the heavy artillery barrage that preceded an offensive, or were gassed into submission, General Henri Gouraud pulled them back, leaving only a thin line holding the forward positions. Once the German infantry moved beyond the forward lines, they came under heavy machine-gun fire and French artillery. They would by then be beyond the range at which their own artillery might have helped.

Consequently Ludendorff's offensive to the east of Rheims was stopped on the first day; to the west of the city some progress—a penetration four miles deep—was made across the Marne to the east of Château-Thierry. Even at this point the drive was stopped by French and American troops on July 16. (General Jean Marie Degoutte, rejecting elastic defense, chose to stock his forward positions strongly with troops.)

246

The battle was still going on when, to the Germans' surprise, Foch launched a counteroffensive on July 18. There was no heralding artillery bombardment; instead hundreds of small French tanks appeared out of the misty woods on the western flank of the Aisne-Marne salient. Followed by American and French troops, they dug into the side of the salient south of Soissons. By the twentieth the Allies began pushing the Germans from all sides; the French took Soissons on August 2. Although many Germans slipped out of the salient, the Allies pushed them back across the Vesle River.

Two days later, on August 8, the British Fourth Army (General Sir Henry Rawlinson), with hundreds of tanks of the British Tank Corps in the vanguard, struck at Ludendorff's bulge threatening Amiens. By evening fifteen miles of the German front, from the Ancre River to the Luce, had buckled to a depth of eight miles.

For the rest of his life Ludendorff referred to August 8 as "the black day of the German army." On that day, after months of nonstop battle, the morale of the German soldier broke. More serious than looting and drinking was the spectacle of entire companies surrendering to a single tank, or retreating troops jeering their comrades marching to the front (16,000 Germans surrendered the first day).

As if that were not enough, Commander-in-Chief Foch proceeded to enkindle the entire Western Front. The pressure on the battle-wearied

Field Marshal Haig and Allied Commander-in-Chief Foch on the Western Front on an inspection tour.

National Archives

Kaiser Wilhelm visits a German command post during the 1918 battles.

German troops hardly lessened at one point before it began at another. British and French armies, one after the other, chewed up the Amiens bulge beginning on August 10. From Arras to Soissons the Germans were driven back, first from the south, then from the north. Overwhelmed, the Germans abandoned the Ypres salient and were driven out of the Somme-Noyon bulge. Ludendorff ordered a withdrawal back to the Hindenburg Line; by September 9 he had lost practically all of the ground won in the costly spring offensive.

Another unsightly bulge in the line, at Saint-Mihiel, in Lorraine south of Verdun, was turned over to the Americans. For the first time the doughboys operated independently as the U. S. First Army under the command of Pershing. The Saint-Mihiel salient had protruded into Lorraine from the beginning of the war; when the Americans attacked—on September 12—the Germans had already thought of leaving it for safer ground. They were too late when the First Army went into action. The Americans were assisted by a massive artillery barrage and some 1,500 aircraft, under the command of air-power prophet Colonel William Mitchell (whose British- and French-made aircraft were manned by Americans, British, and French). At a cost of 7,000 casualties (the

248

German shock troops leaving their trenches in the Third Battle of the Aisne, May 1918.

German soldiers occupying more French ground in the vicinity of the Chemin des Dames. The French have been forced across the Aisne River.

French artillery positions near Soissons before being driven out by the German Seventh Army.

Tank, German version. These monsters carried a crew of 18 "in conditions of acute discomfort" (in the words of Barrie Pitt). Ludendorff was lax in recognizing the value of the tank and no German-made tank appeared on the battlefield until March 1918, in the battle for Lys. Few German tanks were used in the final months of the war.

Battle aftermath: the dead in the wake of the fighting around Cantigny on the Somme. Americans participated for the first time in force at Cantigny.

Germans lost even more) the First Army quickly eliminated the Saint-Mihiel salient and took over 6,000 prisoners and hundreds of guns. It was a small but praiseworthy victory.

With the salients straightened, the Allies again faced the problem of the formidable Hindenburg Line.

The Allies had prepared a series of co-ordinated attacks at various points on the German defensive system. At its southernmost end the French Fourth and the American First armies began moving early in the morning of September 26 in the Meuse-Argonne, west of Verdun. Most of the American troops were inexperienced, since there hadn't been time to transport the "veterans" from Saint-Mihiel for the offensive. The drive, devised primarily to cut the Antwerp-Metz Railroad (over which German troops and supplies had moved for nearly four years), initially went well. The French and Americans enjoyed good air cover and the support of 500 tanks. However, once the Americans got entangled in the

251

Argonne Forest, their end of the drive was checked by stiff resistance and terrain.

As the Meuse-Argonne battle continued, the British First and Third armies struck the line to the north between Lens and Péronne, pushing inexorably toward Cambrai on September 27. On their left flank, the following day, an army group under King Albert of Belgium (commanding Belgian, British, and French divisions) joined the battle. All of Flanders was aflame with gunnery, and Passchendaele, of grim memory, fell again into Allied hands. But so did the rain fall, and, as before, it clogged the advance.

On the day of Albert's attack a dispirited Ludendorff spoke of armistice to Hindenburg; both men hoped to stop the war, if even momentarily, to save their armies. Armistice, not peace, was their concern.

The next day, September 29, the British Fourth and French First armies made a direct assault on the center of the Hindenburg Line. By October 5 a deep wedge had been driven into it, with special hard fighting done by Australian divisions. (Following in the path of untried American troops attached to their corps, the Australians frequently had to fight again for ground that the Americans, who had failed to "mop up," had already taken; once the Americans passed by, the Germans emerged with machine guns and rifles from tunnels and dugouts.)

Although there was forward movement by the Allied line, particularly in the center (the British took Saint-Quentin and Lens in early October), there was also disappointment. To the south the Americans fought desperately and suffered heavy casualties. (When Clemenceau commented on the slow American advance in the Argonne, Foch could only tell him that in four weeks 54,158 doughboys had died, as if the number of dead was any kind of answer to an implied criticism.)

On the northern flank, in Flanders, the weather had slowed the advance as the delivery of supplies and replacements was held up by mud. It appeared as if Foch's Big Push was running out of momentum.

Perhaps, but even so, things were worse on the other side of the Hindenburg Line. Ludendorff exhibited signs of strain and dismay—he was pale (he suffered a mild stroke one afternoon just before a staff meeting); his nerves were gone and it was obvious. He knew, even before the first British troops cracked through the center of the Hindenburg Line on October 5, that the war was lost. He also had known that the Central Powers were cracking everywhere. Even as the British hammered on the Western Front, Germany's allies on the secondary fronts were crumbling.

Bulgaria fell first; after years of near-stalemate, the Macedonian Bird Cage—its political bars cut by the able General Guillaumat—came to life. He had been called back to defend Paris, if need be, during the impending Second Battle of the Marne, and his place was taken by another

U.S. Signal Corps

An American first-aid station directly behind the front; the wounded await evacuation. The American 1st Division has just helped to stop Ludendorff's third offensive of 1918.

Ludendorff's "Black Day." German soldiers marching into captivity after the mass surrenders of August 8, 1918.

Imperial War Museum

able soldier-psychologist, General Louis Franchet d'Esperey, an old-line veteran. Beginning in mid-September, Esperey unleashed his mixed grouping of troops on the demoralized Bulgars and the thinned-out Germans. By the end of September, Bulgaria was out of the war.

The Turks were next in both Mesopotamia and Palestine; the fall of Bulgaria released more British troops to fight the all but defeated Turks. (Earlier in the year Allenby, in Palestine, had lost most of his British troops to the Western Front during Ludendorff's spring offensive.) While Allenby prepared for a September offensive, Lawrence and his Arab band continued to harass the Turks. On September 19, Allenby struck the Turkish (with a few Germans) front on the coastal plain north of Jaffa. The British were expected to attack elsewhere, so the Turks were unprepared and surprised. The British broke the line and soon, in classic style, the cavalry raced through. The Turks were soon in full retreat. By the end of October, in both Palestine and Mesopotamia, the Turks were finished.

Closer to home, on the Austrian-Italian front, Ludendorff must have known since June that ultimate collapse was inevitable. Conrad attempted a double-edged attack on June 13, which ended in failure (and Conrad's ultimate dismissal) and the final drain on Austria's dwindling manpower. When Italian General Diaz went over to the offensive on October 24—the anniversary of the Battle of Caporetto—the outcome was inevitable.

U.S. Signal Corps

American stretcher-bearers remove a wounded man from what was once the town of Vaux.

*A British gun carrier-tank transports a 6-inch howitzer
and crew to a position on the Somme. Foch is about to
launch his counterattack, August 1918.*

*British cavalry on the Arras–Cambrai road on the way to the
front, as wounded soldiers, mostly German, head for the rear. A German
supports a wounded British soldier.*

British artillery moving forward after bypassing a destroyed bridge;
the Germans are being forced back to their Hindenburg Line.

Aided by British, French, and American divisions, Diaz directed the great Battle of Vittorio Veneto, which led to the final dissolution of the Austrian Army and the end of the Hapsburg Empire.

The final agony of the Western Front dragged on despite the outcries for an armistice. In Germany the newly appointed Chancellor, Prince Max of Baden, appealed to President Wilson for an armistice based on the famous "Fourteen Points," i.e., a "peace without victory." During the comparative lull, while notes were exchanged between Berlin and Vienna and Washington (which infuriated certain leaders in London and Paris), Ludendorff regained some of his composure and even began speaking of a spring—1919—offensive! He was also totally unaware of the unrest inside Germany itself.

But the killing continued; and, with the Bulgars and Turks out of the war and the Italians crossing the Piave River, Ludendorff finally resigned, on demand from the Kaiser, as Quartermaster General on October 27. The next day German seamen mutinied at Kiel, refusing to embark on cruiser raids planned by Admiral Scheer; soon crews in Hamburg, Bremen, and Lübeck joined the mutiny. The unrest spread through northwestern Germany.

But the war on the Western Front continued as, painfully, the Allied line pushed forward into Belgium and France, forcing the Germans back toward their homeland. In the north the Belgians again occupied the cities of Bruges and Ghent and, in the center, the British pressed on beyond Cambrai and Saint-Quentin toward the Belgian frontier and, on the right flank of the Allied line, the Americans, bolstered by more seasoned troops, pushed through the horror that had been the Argonne by November 1 and moved forward also. (By this time Pershing had handed the First Army over to Major General Hunter Liggett.)

With Ludendorff forced out by the Kaiser, with Bulgaria and Turkey shattered and Austria on the brink, the new government of Prince Max petitioning for an armistice, and a revolution imminent inside Germany, even the remaining German warlords recognized the pointlessness of continuing with the war. There were even public demands in Berlin to rid Germany of the Kaiser.

As the fighting continued along the Western Front, a German Armistice Commission met with Marshal Foch on November 8 in a railway car on a siding in Compiègne. Two days later, on Hindenburg's advice, the Kaiser, accompanied by the Crown Prince, fled to neutral Holland and sanctuary. On the same day Prince Max, now Regent of the Empire, appointed a Socialist, Friedrich Ebert, Chancellor; a new, democratic German government was promised.

The Germans were unhappy with the armistice that Foch demanded; it would be hard and not sweetened by Wilsonian dreams. But although the fighting would stop officially on November 11, 1918, at 11:00 A.M., it stopped where it began on Belgian and French soil. The Allies had broken the Hindenburg Line but had not invaded Germany itself. The

A section of the Hindenburg Line near Bellicourt (between Cambrai and Saint-Quentin). Allied soldiers study the once formidable obstacle.

British troops, with tank support, prepare to assault the Hindenburg Line.

Moving on, and through, the Hindenburg Line. Ludendorff began talking of an armistice.

strategic bombing of Berlin, planned by Britain's military air pioneer, Hugh Trenchard, was canceled. In short, except for the deprivations caused by the British blockades, Germany had not been touched by the war as had Belgium, France, and Britain. The remnants of the German Army along the front line on November 11 were not, in the exact meaning of the term, defeated in the field. German militarists would later claim that they had not lost the war but had been betrayed by politicians and had suffered "a stab in the back."

By the morning of November 11 the word had gone down that the war would end at eleven that morning. Most of those who had survived were content to dig in, wait, and hope that the word was true, not another rumor. But some German artillery units continued to fire—"every Boche gun between Dommartin and Metz"—on Americans in the Saint-Mihiel sector. The Americans returned in kind.

Some overzealous American commanders fought to the last minute in a pointless race with the French to take Sedan, contributing only some last-minute names to the casualty toll. Some German units waited too, but others fought savagely to the final moment. When some horsemen of the British Seventh Dragoons, perhaps for old times' sake, decided to stage a last cavalry charge upon a bridge at Lessines, they galloped straight into a machine-gun nest at 10:50 A.M. In accordance with the order of the day, the guns stopped precisely at eleven.

A German pillbox after Allied artillery bombardment. This emplacement housed several machine guns.

The state of the German Army is obvious in this photo of a prisoner taken by the American 128th Infantry near Montfaucon in October. Fourteen days after this boy was drafted he was in battle and then in enemy custody.

In another British sector, in a tiny Belgian village, a British patrol came upon a wounded German officer awaiting medical attention, who informed the patrol leader that the Germans had evacuated the village hours before. Assured, the British following the patrol formed up and

260

marched into the village—and were machine-gunned from several carefully placed nests. Over a hundred British fell before their comrades killed all the Germans they could find—including the German officer who had tricked them into the trap.

An unnatural silence finally fell over the Western Front and the slaughter ended. The quiet was as dazzling as the final barrages. Soldiers emerged from their holes and stared upon the devastation of a world made safe for democracy. Ten million human beings had perished in that war (and twice that number suffered wounds) and the costs in goods manufactured and destroyed was an astronomical $180,500,000,000 merely for the expense of running the war itself; an additional $151.6 billion could be added as "indirect costs" in lost business, etc. The numbers are of such magnitude they are virtually meaningless—as, indeed, was the Great War itself.

Aftermath: During the treaty negotiations at Versailles in 1919, one of the German delegates said to French Prime Minister Clemenceau, "I

The Armistice came a week too late for this German machine gunner, who died at his post near Villers devant Dun on November 4, 1918.

Prisoner-of-war clearing station, Abbeville, France.
The Allies were taking German prisoners wholesale in
the final drives of the war.

wonder what history will have to say about all this?" The old "Tiger"
curtly replied, "History will not say Belgium invaded Germany."

Clemenceau was in no mood for speculation but intent on avenging
the death and destruction the war had brought to his country. He, along
with Lloyd George and Wilson, dominated the hammering out of the
Treaty of Versailles—and frequently they disagreed on the terms. Wilson's idealistic Fourteen Points went out the window and harsh terms
were laid down: loss of German colonies, heavy reparation, disarma-

262

Parisians celebrate the announcement of the Armistice.

ment, stringent limitations on German military establishments (including no air force and no submarine command), and a "war guilt" clause, placing all the blame for the war on Germany. The German delegation signed only under protest: The United States Congress refused to ratify it, in defiance of Wilson and in rejection of a proposed League of Nations that would, it was felt, continue to entangle America in European affairs. In Britain and France, public opinion opposed the treaty because it was not harsh enough.

Meanwhile Germany was racked by pro-Communist revolutionaries threatening the new government; the German General Staff went underground, already making plans to avenge the "stab in the back." Inflation further added to the misery and unrest. The Allies took up the task of peace-keeping along the Rhine River. They hardly knew what transpired inside Germany as the weak democratic government became entrapped by the militarists (as wily General Hans von Seeckt secretly rebuilt the German Army) and was plagued by dissidents, many of them former soldiers and sailors who felt abused and betrayed (among them an insignificant corporal named Adolf Hitler). In Berlin it took a basket of money to buy one loaf of bread while the Allies demanded large reparations.

Allied troops—French, British, and American—were sent to Russia

263

to put down the Bolsheviks. The specter of communism was haunting Europe, indeed, and the Allies preferred a White government to a Red. Before they left Russia in October 1919 they left many dead Reds behind them. The new Russian regime would long remember that.

Nor would the Germans forget what had been done to them at Versailles (any more than the French forgot their racked land, cities, and villages, and both Britain and France mourned the death of an entire generation). So it was that November 11, 1918, was not the beginning of the end; it was merely the end of the beginning.

National Archive

Hall of Mirrors, Versailles, where the Versailles Treaty was hammered out, including the clause assigning "war guilt" to the Germans. The Germans signed under protest. The seeds for the next war were planted at Versailles.

Commander-in-Chief of the recovered French Army, General
Pétain (center) inspects his troops poised to meet the
German spring offensive. To Pétain's left, Prime Minister Georges
Clemenceau; behind him, General Maxime Weygand, Foch's chief of staff.

German shock troops move through a French town; such troops
could bypass strongpoints, leaving them for larger units,
and deal with snipers.

*Holding the line on the Somme: French and British
soldiers in rifle pits await the oncoming Germans. Mixed
units such as this were not very successful because
of the language barrier.*

*A German shell lands near a British artillery unit,
Battle of Lys, April 1918.*

British wounded moving to the rear during the Lys Offensive; Ludendorff's soldiers did not succeed in taking Hazebrouck.

Paris street scene, the result of German shelling.

A mobile machine-gun unit, the British 24th Motor Machine Gun Battalion, lined up for inspection, June 1918; the German drive on the Aisne was ending.

Free ride: Canadian troops enjoy a brief outing between German offensives, riding atop a British tank. This Mark IV weighed twenty-six tons, spouted six guns, was operated by a crew of eight, and had a top speed of not quite 4 mph.

British soldiers inspect a German tank trap they have overrun;
one checks the battlefield with a trench periscope.

British aircraft, in an Alpine setting, assist the Italians
in driving the Austrians out of the war. The Bristol
fighters were capable of strafing troops or dropping light
(20-pound) bombs on them.

*Out of the Bird Cage of Macedonia. Bulgarian troops on the
run. Bulgaria was the first of Germany's allies to sign
an armistice with the Allied powers, September 1918.*

*The war continues on the Western Front: a British armored
car with ambulance evacuates the wounded; in the background,
a horse-drawn ambulance.*

*French cavalrymen examine an abandoned German position
in Flanders. A trench mortar is in the foreground;
a gas alarm horn is affixed to a log,
to the left of the shells and at
the forefeet of the horse.*

*An American balloon company
moves to the front,
October 1918.*

*British breaking through the center of the Hindenburg Line
in the Battle of Saint-Quentin Canal.*

*Protective cover: a ditched tank provides shelter from
German gunfire for British troops pushing toward Cambrai.*

*A Canadian patrol enters the battered French town of
Cambrai, October 9, 1918. The Germans are abandoning their
strongholds in France and Belgium.*

German arms taken during the British advance on Cambrai.

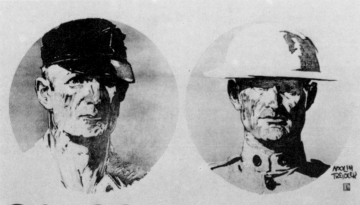

The COMBINATION
THAT WILL WIN the WAR

Every piece of work done in this plant has a direct bearing on the outcome of the war.
Our finished product goes to France.
The men who face for us weariness, hardships, death, depend upon us.
Our work here, fits their work over there, like a cog in a giant machine.
Without our product they are helpless. With it they are invincible.
They fight with what we make. We are their resource and reliance, the American workman and the American soldier, the combination that will win the war.

A poster displayed in a munitions plant extolling the workmen to do their best for the Boys Over There.

The Yanks have arrived. American soldiers and British W.A.A.C.'s meeting in France.

Commander-in-Chief of the Allied Armies Foch and American commande Pershing in a friendly moment. Pershing insisted that American troops serve under American commanders and refused to permit Foch to dole the out to British and French leaders.

4592

*A light moment as Pershing fraternizes with members of the
French High Command. Foch is to Pershing's right (the lady
is not identified, nor is the child); Joffre looms between
the lady and the child. General Auguste Dubail, once commander
of the French First Army, stands at far right, front row.*

*American women served in the Army during World War I;
Signal Corps telephone operators in France, 1918.*

*The doughboy's nemesis: a German observation balloon, which
they called a sausage. These floated along the front lines
to bring the soldiers under accurate artillery fire.*

*A royal welcome: King George V greets the American 30th
Division, assigned to bolster the British during the fighting on
the Aisne, July–August 1918. With the King is the division's
newly appointed commander, Major General Edward M. Lewis.*

Always a welcome sight at the front: an observation balloon shot down by a fighter plane—in this instance an American balloon shot down by a German plane.

An American rations train on the way to the front.

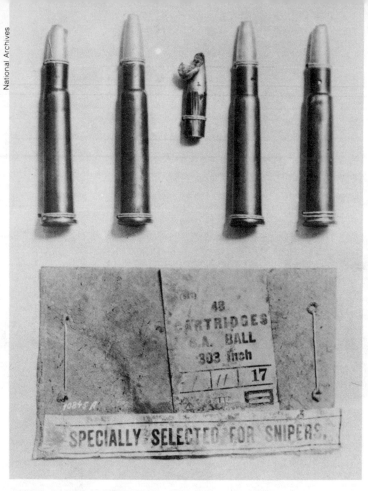

The hated "dumdum" bullet. This German photograph
was circulated to prove that the English were using
cartridges with the tips cut off. These inflicted
very serious wounds and were outlawed by the Geneva
Conventions. (The name came from Dum-Dum, India, where
these bullets were tested for the first time.)

Mechanized war: a German grenade launcher. A man was no longer
required to throw it by hand into an enemy trench.

German soldiers are placing carrier pigeons in a gas-proof shelter. Although radios and telephones were used for communication, pigeons were widely used as message carriers in the front lines.

German shock troops (advance troops that infiltrated through Allied positions wreaking havoc) and the tools of their trade, various forms of hand grenades. Grenades, too, like the dumdum bullet, produced frightful, difficult-to-heal wounds. They were regarded as perfectly acceptable weapons of civilized warfare.

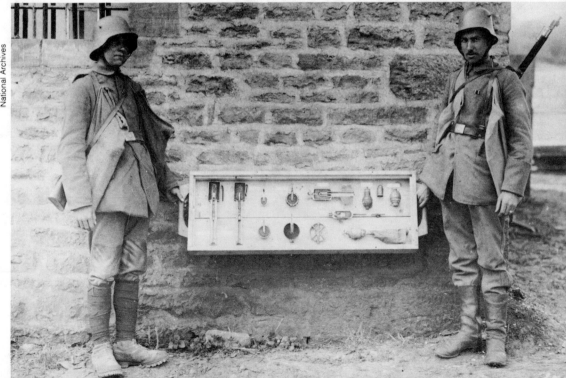

U.S. Air Force

The beginning of a gas attack. This could be done only if the wind were blowing in the direction of enemy lines; and a shift in wind direction could backfire. Although not truly effective, gas could be devastating and was dreaded by soldiers.

National Archives

An appeal for the increased production of gas masks, 1918.

This posed photo was used to demonstrate the effect of phosgene gas on the soldier who neglected to wear his mask. After the war it was widely distributed as an actual battlefield picture.

Rewards for courage: Pershing decorates a private of the 2nd Division, while, on the right, no fewer than three generals await their turn.

*The gadget fastened to the rifle barrel, just below
the bayonet, when activated spewed flame at the enemy
soldier. It was a weapon that seems to have fallen
by the wayside of war, but it is an example of how
war inspires man's fiendish imagination.*

*A French Renault light tank, called the Mosquito. It
carried a crew of two, one of whom was the gunner. These
tanks are operating with American troops.*

The last act begins. The Allied offensive on the Somme, September 1918.
German machine-gun crews are dug in and waiting.

A German observation post on the Somme, 1918.

Members of the "Harlem Hellfighters," 369th Regiment, an all-black, all-volunteer unit that served with the French 16th Division. The unit lost half of its men in the final weeks of the war. The Hellfighters were in front-line combat longer than any other American unit. The French awarded them no fewer than 171 Croix de Guerre.

Life, Liberty and Happiness.

So long as the Administration is determined to keep the war going there is only one way for you to get out of this miserable fix and that is for you to stop fighting. You can do this honourably. As a free born American citizen you have the right to

life, liberty and the pursuit of happiness.

The American constitution guarantees to you these rights. **Exercise them!**

Get out and dash to safety! If you don't, you stand a very slim chance of ever seeing Broadway or the old home again.

The Wall Street millionaires may like this war, because they are becoming billionaires. But you will have to pay for it all, my boy,

pay for it with your blood and taxes

and the tears of your loved ones at home.

If you were fighting on your own soil against a foreign foe it would be another matter, but what are you doing in Europe? France is not your country, neither is Belgium nor Alsace Lorraine. Are you satisfied that you are in the full enjoyment of your "inalienable rights to life, liberty and the pursuit of happiness" as promised to you by the

American bill of rights.

The years will be lean and weary and the work will be hard and long for you and the longer the war lasts the longer will be the debt which you will have to pay to the money magnates of Wall Street for the munitions you are shooting away.

Don't give up your life till you have to and don't give any more labor for the **benefit of the money trust!** Quit it!

German propaganda leaflet scattered by aircraft over the front lines, inviting American soldiers to surrender and providing the reasons for not fighting.

A German poster appealing for funds
for German prisoners of war. The
artist: Ludwig Hohlwein. Through the
Red Cross, prisoners were provided
with packages of food, clothing, and
simple luxuries such as soap.

German photo posed to show the range of nationalities fighting, and being captured by, the Germans. From left: Annamite, Tunisian, Senegalese, Sudanese,
Russian, American, Portuguese, and English.

*Contraband: a German prisoner of war in France received a
loaf of bread from home (Germany to Switzerland to France);
inside the bread was a walnut containing a letter. This
was one means of communicating directly with a loved one.*

**The final push on the Western Front is on; an American
machine-gun company of the 1st Division moving forward.**

*American long-range artillery (a 14-inch gun) pounds
at German positions twenty miles away.*

*An American artillery battery
commander, Captain Harry Truman
of the 35th Division, which saw
action in the Meuse-Argonne.*

An American tank stuck in the mud.

Keeping the Germans on the run; an American field artillery battery during the Meuse-Argonne offensive, near Varennes.

Yank ingenuity. American engineers install barbed wire in the wake of the Allied advance. Fencelike construction was an innovation.

German wounded at an American dressing station during the Meuse-Argonne offensive.

Doughboys marching past the Crown Prince's former headquarters at Montfaucon.

*Supplies for the front jammed up in the town of Esnes,
beyond which lay the jump-off line in the Argonne
push. The traffic moved at a rate of 2 mph.*

*Improvised hospital—a battle-scarred church at Neuilly during
the American drive through the Argonne. The dead have not
been removed from among those who are still living. Soldier
(lower center) contemplates the bodies of three buddies.*

*Front line at Forges. Men of the 132nd Infantry, 33rd Division,
dug in within view of the Meuse River, October 1918.*

*Across the Meuse. Engineers cross the river on their
newly constructed footbridge with materials for the construction
of a larger bridge for vehicles and troops.*

*Infantry of the 27th Division advance through a pathway
cut through German barbed wire by a tank. One soldier,
at right, has been hit.*

Out of the trenches and into the streets. As the Allied
offensive gained momentum, the fighting moved rapidly through
French towns and villages, sometimes dangerously from house
to house. The Germans frequently left small machine-gun
units behind to cover their withdrawal.

Running for cover under shellfire. A medical corpsman (center) had
been attending the German soldier, who is obviously dead.

Australians, with tank support, move through the Hindenburg Line.

*American Ace of Aces, Edward V. Rickenbacker, who finished the war
with a victory "score" of twenty-six enemy aircraft. He is seated in the cockpit
of his Spad. Rickenbacker eventually became commanding officer of the
94th Aero Squadron.*

Brigadier General William Mitchell (second from left, seated), who replaced Foulois as chief air officer of the First Army. Mitchell brought order out of the chaos of the Air Service's organization and co-operated with the Allies in planned air attacks in force.

Brigadier General Benjamin Foulois and General Pershing at the Aviation Training Center at Issoudon, France. Foulois had been Chief of Air Service, A.E.F., but Pershing, unhappy with his performance, made him Chief of Air Service, First Army. His replacement—General Mason M. Patrick, an engineer who had never before been in an airplane—led the American air effort in France.

Yankee Doodle Dandy. Brigadier General Douglas MacArthur, at age 38, the commander of the legendary 42nd (Rainbow) Division. The Rainbow was made up of men from all over the U.S., thus the popular name. MacArthur proved himself a skilled field commander on the Western Front.

*The war in the air was a concept introduced during World War I.
Fighting airmen were lionized during the war, and tales of their exploits
were in newspapers and magazines—and, after the war, in books and films.
Few people had ever experienced vistas like this above the clouds, as a
British Armstrong Whitworth purportedly pursues a German Fokker
over the front.*

*Manfred von Richthofen, German Ace
of Aces (eighty victories) was undoubtedly
the most publicized airman of the war.
His death in April 1918 was cause for
mourning in Germany and he was
given a hero's funeral by his former
enemies. Richthofen shot down more
planes than any other combat pilot of
the war. This is a copy of a German
postcard of him.*

Hermann Goering, a high-scoring German ace, was given the command of Richthofen's squadron after the great ace's death and until the war's end. Goering later became the head of the Luftwaffe.

The legendary Fokker Triplane, the type that Richthofen was flying when he was shot down (by either Canadian pilot Roy Brown or an Australian machine gunner on the ground—still a controversy). The plane had a dramatic appearance, especially when colorfully decorated, but it suffered structural failures and sometimes came fluttering down with folded wings. It was highly maneuverable in combat.

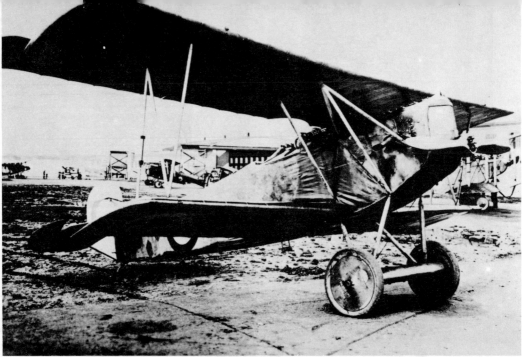

The Fokker D.VII, a fighter introduced after the Triplane and a much superior aircraft. Luckily for the Allies, it came too late to make much difference in the outcome of the war.

The war was decided on the ground—most military commanders of World War I had little understanding of military aircraft. In this photo, curious doughboys gather around a German Fokker D.VII that had been shot down behind the lines.

Pushing the Germans out of France. U. S. Marines, with a 37-mm. gun, advance through a blasted wood.

Cracking from within: the German fleet, which began to mutiny at Wilhelmshaven in October, initiated the revolt inside Germany. A submarine prepares to hoist the white flag of surrender in a German port.

A German ship surrenders to the Woolsey.

*Berlin, November 10, 1918—on the eve of the signing of the
Armistice. Soldiers, sailors, and civilians on Unter den Linden;
the Kaiser has already left for sanctuary in Holland.*

German soldiers, wearing the armband of rebellion and mutiny, take an antigovernment stand in Berlin.

Pro-government troops on patrol in the streets of Berlin during the uprising.

A German field gun in the courtyard of the Royal Palace,
Berlin. It was eventually occupied by the revolutionaries
of the Soldiers' Council.

Defeated German troops returning to Berlin; the war is over.
Though defeated, Germany did not suffer from Allied invasion,
bombardment, or bombing from the air. The banner hanging
in the arch of the Brandenburg Gate reads "Friede
und Freiheit" (*Peace and Freedom*).

Paris, November 11, 1918—awaiting word of the signing of the Armistice.

Georges Clemenceau, Prime Minister of France at the time of the Armistice. Nicknamed "The Tiger," Clemenceau presided at the Paris Peace Conference in 1919.

Journey's end: Allied warplanes, junked and ready for the torch, in the belief that indeed World War I had been the war to end all wars.

Watch on the Rhine. An American soldier on guard on the Rhine to assure German adherence to the Versailles Treaty. The terms of the treaty were poorly enforced, and the German military began rebuilding its army and air force under the noses of the Inter-Allied Commission of Control. Allied occupation was minimal.

A postwar dedication of a memorial to the Battle of Tannenberg attended by World War I notables—(left to right) Mackensen, Ludendorff, Hindenburg, Seeckt. In a few years Ludendorff allied himself with Adolf Hitler, who was bent on avenging the Versailles Treaty. Hindenburg, President of the German Republic in 1925, named Hitler Chancellor in 1933. Meanwhile, Seeckt, with Soviet aid, rebuilt the German Army, emphasizing the Air Force and mobile tank units. This gave birth to a method of making war known as Blitzkrieg.

INDEX

INDEX

INDEX